Lynn Roby Meekins

The Robb's Island Wreck

And Other Stories

Lynn Roby Meekins

The Robb's Island Wreck
And Other Stories

ISBN/EAN: 9783744714365

Printed in Europe, USA, Canada, Australia, Japan

Cover: Foto ©Thomas Meinert / pixelio.de

More available books at **www.hansebooks.com**

THE

ROBB'S ISLAND WRECK

AND OTHER STORIES

BY

LYNN R. MEEKINS

CHICAGO AND CAMBRIDGE

STONE AND KIMBALL

MDCCCXCIV

CONTENTS.

THE ROBB'S ISLAND WRECK.

I.

THEY began by having great fun with the captain. Ten minutes before they arrived the captain came out and took his usual chair in the usual spot under the shadow of the station. He was not a handsome man. He was strong, rugged, picturesque, but not handsome. Six feet high and two hundred pounds in weight, he was an epic in hardened flesh and muscle. His face was as full of lines as an etched portrait. His general appearance offered a contrast to every rule of a fashion-plate, and he appeared like some big shaggy animal that was particularly lazy because it was especially strong.

On this occasion the captain's eyes were half-reefed, and they looked over an expanse of sand on which low houses were built, and saw the smoke of passing steamers that crept along the horizon. It was peaceful, but it was n't much of a view.

In fact Robb's Island was n't much of a place; simply a few hundred acres of sand in a wilderness of salt water. But it had its fascinations. For instance, in summer, people — some of them of such good family stock that they did n't have to talk about it — left their best clothes and formalities at home and went there. They lived in rough sheds, by courtesy collectively called a hotel, fished in the inlets, tumbled around in the surf, waded through the ever-shifting sand, and gathered flesh and tan and strength and freckles on the worst food that a summer resort could possibly offer. At first Robb's Island was deeply disappointing. You reached the place in a stuffy little boat, after a sail of ten miles from the mainland. The commonness and the glare of everything disgusted you. You firmly resolved to return the next morning. But the boat did n't go for two days, and there you were! In those two days you got into the surf, and pulled up more fish than you ever saw before, caught a shark or two, became the owner of a wonderful appetite, and when the boat was ready to start, you were on the other side of the island. In a week you were a confirmed victim to the repose of the place, and you remained a hopeless islander until your conscience or your finances drove you across the ten miles of marsh and water to the world and its cares.

After the summer visitors went away in September, parties of men with canvas clothes and big guns arrived to kill ducks and geese; and when they departed, the island, with its hundred people, was left alone in the solitude of the waters. There was not much to do then, and the inhabitants did it. It was a dull life and a dull place. Everybody was well, and the only way to break the monotony was for the women folks to imagine a few complaints to fit the descriptions in the patent-medicine almanacs. A small community without sick people to gossip about is stupid, but the best that Robb's Island could do was to manufacture petty aches, and doctor them on home-made remedies. The idea of a resident physician was preposterous. He would n't make enough in a year to feed a cat on bread-crumbs and water, much less milk.

The most interesting place on the island was the life-saving station, — a fine house of two stories, with a broad gable roof, a flag-staff, a veranda, and a liberal decoration of red paint, whose contagion had spread over the neighborhood, and given the settlement a sanguinary hue. The keeper of the station and the captain of the life-saving crew, who, according to the authorities, are two gentlemen at once, at four hundred dollars a year for the total, was, and is, Captain Zebedee Graves; and on this afternoon he had eaten his dinner, and was trying to smoke and sleep and keep his eyes open at the same time. He almost succeeded, but he was losing himself in furtive naps when other men began to come out. At first they did n't disturb him. They took seats, quietly stretched their limbs, and gazed across the expanse of sand and sea. The captain dozed; then the six surfmen looked at one another and smiled.

The smallest man struck a match and lighted his pipe. He puffed twice, threw his hands over his knees, rocked backwards and forwards several times, and began to speak. "Gentlemen," he said, "this life 's getting too slow. I think I 'll go ashore, and let some nice girl with a farm marry me, — a girl or a widder; I guess I 'll take a widder."

There was a pause. The captain's eyes opened one-thousandth part of an inch. The other men looked into vacancy. The captain said nothing.

"You 'd better be quick about it, then," advised the long man. "From what I hear, widders is mighty popular now, and somebody might cut you out."

"Oh, I guess not," said the short man. "Good goods come in little bundles, and widders know quality. Don't they, captain?"

The captain's eyes opened another fraction, and he took his pipe from his mouth and growled, "What are you up to now?"

"Oh, nothing. I just thought of going ashore and getting some things, and calling on a widder."

"Then why don't you go?"

"I 'm afraid somebody 's got ahead of me."

The men langhed, and the captain scowled, and took an extra puff from his pipe.

The long man spoke up: "You need n't try to deny it, captain. We 've got the dead wood on you this time."

And then followed volleys of questions from all the six men. They wanted to know when the marriage was to take place, when he was going to bring his bride over, and whether or not they would receive invitations to the ceremony. The captain puffed away at his pipe, but behind the smoke was an increasing exasperation. The boys welcomed the signs with undisguised glee. The truth of the matter was that the captain aroused was one of their greatest delights. They often said that they would rather hear him swear than the church choir sing; and they never thought it a sin, because the oaths — which, of course, cannot get their natural glow in repetition — seemed to be an inevitable part of the man. He stood their prodding longer than they expected, but finally he blurted out something which, considerably expurgated, amounted to this: —

"What if I did go to see the widder? Is it any of your business? If people would attend to their own affairs this here world would be a heap better off. I 'd get married if I wanted to; but, thunderation! who wants to get married? I would n't marry a angel if she was to come down and ask me, 'specially if I had to introduce her to some good-for-nothing loafers that I know of."

"We 're not talking about angels, captain, but widders, which is altogether different."

"You jaw about marriage as if it was a joke," continued the captain, ignoring the interruption. "It ain't a joke, it 's serious;

and it ruins more men than whiskey. Men don't know their own minds till they are forty, and then they mostly stay single; but if one does marry, he generally picks out the right sort of wife. What's the matter with the world now? What caused all this hard work and this starvation pay? What but an early marriage? If Adam had had the sense to wait for another woman, he'd 'a' done something in the world a little better than stealing apples."

"But, captain," put in the long man, who had married when he was eighteen, "there are —"

"Of course there is. I don't say nothing about present company. There's a few married men who's all right, and there's a big lot who ain't worth a cupful of salt water. And yonder's one of 'em."

The men turned, and about four hundred yards away saw a heavily built young fellow with hatchet and nails mending the fence that enclosed a small and neatly kept two-story house. The countenance of every one in the party fell — every one except the captain. He ground his teeth and sneered.

"That's a nice married man for you; a nice land-lubberly piece of dough and fresh water he is!"

"Now, captain, you 've no right to talk against Henry that way. You know that he resigned because he had the heart-disease. You know —"

"Tom Thorpe, I know more about Henry Dane in a minute than you do in a year, and I say he 's a lazy loafer. Who brought that boy up? I did, d—— him! Who taught him to be the strongest helmsman and the best all-round life-saver on the island? Who got him a place in this crew? I did, and you all know it. When he wanted to get married, I said no; not that I had nothing agin the woman, but she was a woman, and if Tom was to take my place, he had no right to get married. But married he got; and what come of it? Why, pretty soon he had the heart-disease. Bah!"

"Be fair, captain. There ain't a braver man on the island than Henry," said the tall surfman. "We all saw him keel over out there in the surf no less than four times."

"What if he did?" growled the captain. "Hain't I been knocked out a dozen times? That don't show nothing. He passed the examination, did n't he?"

"But it was n't very strict in his case," answered the long man.

"It was strict enough. There ain't no sickness on this island — you know that — and Henry was the soundest boy here till he got married, and then his wife and that doctor who was down here last summer made him believe that something ailed his heart, and told him he had to get out of the service or die. And he got out, d—— him! he got out. And I hain't spoke to him since, and I would n't if he was on his dying bed. Every hope I had was wrapped up in that boy. He'd 'a' been keeper of this station; and look at him now, a big calf yoked to two apron strings! Heart failure, is it? I tell you it's nerve failure — that's what it is."

Never were six men more miserable. They tried to defend their comrade, but it was useless. Each word increased the captain's anger. Presently there was silence. He puffed at his pipe; they tried to look at ease.

"Now I guess you want to know why I went to see the Widder Marling," resumed the captain, with something like contempt in his voice. "She's a cousin of Joe Black, who happens to be at the head of things over in the county just now, and the doctor says she must come to Robb's Island for her health, and she wants something to do while she is here. So she 's going to teach the school."

The miserable men were no longer quiet. They started as if a bomb-shell had dropped in their midst.

"You don't mean to say, captain, that she 's going to take the place of Henry's wife?" stammered Tom.

"That 's exactly what I mean."

Every man had something to say in indignant protest.

"It 's no use to kick," answered the captain to them all. "The thing 's settled. We done enough for Henry in giving him the place here, and he throwed it up. His wife don't belong to the island, and as he married her, let him support her. I 've got no hard feelings agin her, but the bosses over in the county say Mrs. Marling must have the place, and she 's got it, and I 've been to see her about moving over."

It was an ill ending to the joke of the jokers. They were too depressed to talk, and gradually they got up and moved away.

II.

SOME people still talk about the November storm of that year. It sent more than forty boats ashore, and for hours it kept many of the one hundred and sixty-five life-saving stations along the Atlantic coast in constant readiness and apprehension. Had it not been for the work of the life-savers, more than a hundred souls would have perished; but in the face of cold and death these brave fellows risked everything, and played the rôles of heroes with as splendid a courage and as honest a purpose as ever the world saw. The great public, with its twelve-hour memory, read the brief reports in the newspapers the next morning, and then promptly forgot all about it by dinner-time.

On Robb's Island the day began queerly. A yellowish sunshine disfigured the morning. By nine o'clock thick, deep, dark clouds were rolling along the horizon, and by noon a heavy wind, uncertain in its direction, was beating the waves into whiteness, and piling up the blackness of the heavens. Rain poured down in big drops, and fell faster than the porous sand could receive it. Then there was a lull, and by and by came a deluge from above, driven by the wind into every crevice, and forcing everything animate to a refuge. In the life-saving station the men looked out of the windows and smoked — and smoked and looked out of the windows. The first regular watch was at sunset, but the sun was behind an ocean of ink, and by the time it got below the horizon, twilight changed to night, and the rain turned into a bombardment of hail, that rattled on the roof like a fusillade of infantry bullets.

Just about that time the small man came into the room in oil-skins and rubbers.

"Rough night, Tom," said the captain.

"Yes, captain. I don't think it'll be very dusty on the sands to-night. Perhaps some of you fellows would like to take the walk?"

"Glad you think so," said the long man.

"Well, never mind. I 'm rather thinking you 'll all get baptized before morning. The shoals look ugly, and if any boat gets in too close, may the good Lord help her! Good night, gentlemen."

"Good-night, Tom."

The patrol on Robb's Island was different from that of the ordinary coast station. The stretch of beach being less than two miles, only one patrolman was needed during a watch. Tom was the first man out. He carried his lantern and the Coston signals. The hail having turned to snow, the light of the lantern reached but a short distance, and beyond that was utter darkness. In ordinary weather the walk was not bad, but that night it was a sorry journey. The violence of the wind increased enormously. It was as if the storm god was using the air as a herculean lash to whip nature into chaos, and was wielding it right and left, backward and forward, with gigantic recklessness. More than once the poor fellow fell, but he was soon up again, fighting his way along the sands. You, my dear sir, with your comfortable bank account, would n't have stayed out there for forty dollars an hour. This surfman — thanks to the munificence of the richest government on the earth — was doing it for forty dollars a month.

In four hours he was back at the station, and another unfortunate was sent forth to make the round. After four hours he came back, half-drowned and exhausted. Then another set out in the face of the storm, and a weary time he had of it; but he stumbled along against the tempest, going down frequently, but soon rising, and all the time gazing seawards, with his Coston signal ready to warn any ill-starred mariner.

As calculated afterwards, it was sixty-five minutes before the break of day when this patrolman thought he saw the glimmer of a light a half-mile beyond the shoals. He climbed on a bluff of sand and looked again, but the snow fell thick and fast, and he could see nothing. Suddenly he heard a cry. He was sure of it, and then, settling all doubt, came the report of a gun. Before its echo had answered the sound, he ignited the Coston signal.

For two minutes its brilliant red flame illuminated the storm. And then he struck another, and for two minutes more the warning glare burned forth, and from the dark water came a second report of the gun.

The patrolman turned at once, and ran as fast as he could towards the station.

Somehow the captain had not slept that night. His thoughts were on the sea. His eyes were looking out towards the window. He heard the muffled echo of the gun, and thought he saw the glare of the signal.

He jumped up and shouted, in a voice louder than the roar of the angry surf, "Get out, everybody!"

There was a stampede, a rush down the steps, a swinging open of the big doors, and in a twinkling the surf-boat, resting gracefully on its four-wheeled carriage and drawn by the six men, had rumbled down the incline, and was on its way towards the beach.

The snow was deep and the sand was deeper, and the work was hard, but the six men had muscles of iron and wills of steel, and they pulled the load of nearly a thousand pounds as if they were horses trained for the work. No one spoke except the captain, and his vociferous tones rose above the storm and urged the men to their best endeavor.

The same tones reached the houses on the island, and in a short time the whole population was aroused. No one thought of cold, or of the snow, or of pneumonia; there was a wreck, and a wreck would call a dying Robb's-Islander from the portals of the grave. So out the people came, with untied shoes and unbuttoned garments, running pell-mell across the sands, and trying to overtake the life-saving crew.

The crew were several hundred yards ahead, and were making good progress. By that time, too, the patrolman had met his comrades, and was pulling with them at the ropes of the carriage. They needed his assistance, for the sand dunes were getting larger, and the work was growing heavier, and the captain was swearing harder. A hundred yards more, and the half-dressed islanders caught up with the crew, and lent their willing aid to the men.

Day was just breaking when they reached the point opposite the wreck. In the uncertain light they saw a schooner stuck fast on the shoals. The heavy seas were pounding her sides and throwing cataracts of water across her decks. No vessel could long endure such violence, and already pieces of wreckage were reaching the shore, showing that she was breaking up. She was too far out for the guns and the breeches buoy. The only hope was the surf-boat, and between her and the crew were the great shoals covered with prodigious breakers, whipped into whiteness by the fury of the wind, and full of uncertain currents and death-sweeping undertows.

"The boat can't live in that sea," said a voice in the crowd.

"Live?" roared the captain. "She 's got to live!"

The half-dressed islanders shivered. Some of the women, whose husbands or sons were surfmen, sobbed aloud. The captain turned his head a second to look at them, and as he did so his eyes fell on Henry Dane, who, pale but calm, was standing with his wife watching the crew fix the carriage for the launching of the boat. Across the captain's face swept a wave of indignant disgust. Henry saw it and felt it.

But minutes were hours then, and there was no time for anything but the work of rescue.

"Ready, captain," said Tom.

The captain leaped into the stern, and grabbed the long steering-oar. The six surfmen, obedient and watchful, waited for the sign. A great wave rolled in, and on its recession the boat glided into the turbulent surf. Down she dropped and up she came, again she fell and again she rose, but as she rested on the wave's crest, another breaker, driven diagonally by the uncertain wind, slashed her side, hid her in its spray, and turned her prow from its course. With magnificent skill the Hercules in the stern sought to swing her back, but the forces of hell itself were in those breakers, and the vantage lost, human skill was not enough. Before the oar could get a second hold on the water, a great maddening cascade, larger and stronger than all the rest, picked up the boat as if she were a child's plaything, and tossed her angrily towards the shore.

The men on land ran forward and helped the surfmen get the boat back on the sand. And they brought with her the form of the captain, his right arm powerless, and blood streaming from a deep gash across his temple.

Henry Dane saw all this. He saw what the broken wrist meant. He saw the grounded vessel giving way to the pounding of the waves. He saw that the lives upon her had to be saved at any cost. There in the stern he would be at home, — he whom the captain had taught, whom the boys had trusted. So intent were his thoughts that he scarcely felt the clinging of the woman at his side — of her who was more to him than all the world — scarcely heard her words imploring him not to go.

"We need another man," hallooed Tom.

Henry looked at the trembling form of his wife, and unclasped her hands from his arm.

"It 's my duty; I must," he said.

"Then go," she replied; "and may God keep you!"

He sprang forward. In an instant he was in the stern, with the steering-oar balanced for its work. There were no cheers, no demonstrations from the islanders. It was Henry's place to go, and he went; that was all. And, moreover, most of the folks were around the prostrate captain, binding up his wounds, and holding him down.

The surfmen and their new captain saw nothing, knew nothing, but the work ahead of them. As Henry stood at his post the whiteness left his face, and all the old earnestness rushed back to warm his blood, to strengthen his muscle.

It seemed like the old days to the surfmen to hear him sing out: "Steady now, boys. Here comes a bully one. One, two, three, *let her go!*"

She went. Into the seething turbulence she fell, and on the snowy crest she rose. Henry held her true and straight. He profited by the captain's failure; calculated for the diagonal waves, and with firm nerve and splendid strength guided her through the dangers of the breakers. His loud voice rose above the storm.

"Strong there, Tom. There 's a whopper. All together, boys. That 's past. Now we 're all right."

The men never pulled more magnificently, and the boat, obedient to the helmsman's touch, leaped from wave to wave, carrying the prayers of those on shore, the hopes of the freezing wretches on the wreck.

And yet she seemed to go slowly—oh, so slowly! The captain, his left eye hid by the rough cloths which were bound around his wound, arose and looked.

"God bless the boy!" he said.

And the people thought the boy needed it, for the boat was often hidden by the spray, and it looked as if she could not live through the trip. But when they saw Henry standing steadfastly at his post, the men working the oars like machines, and the whole crew fighting the storm inch by inch towards the vessel, they took hope, and believed that he would conquer. It was a half-hour of indescribable suspense, a half-hour that seemed a whole day, but at the end of it the surf-boat was nearer the vessel's side.

Three times she tried to approach the wreck, and three times the waves swept her away; and as failure followed failure, the five men and the boy on the vessel seemed to give up hope. But not so Henry. The fourth time success came, and in a minute the six castaways jumped aboard, and nestled there in speechless joy.

All knew the perils of the trip ashore.

Progress was easier, but the dangers were greater. Henry was exuberant no longer. His face was grim, not boyish, and the paleness came back. For a while the boat cut swiftly through the sea, leaping from breaker to breaker with splendid speed. But when she reached the cut-off channel that ran between the shore and the shoals the serious work began. The beach seemed only a few yards away, but between it and the boat more than one tragedy had ended the hopes of sailors in bygone years. Henry knew it well. Just as the boat plunged into it, a hidden current tried to pull her to her death; but he was quick, and the boat was brought back to her course. A minute more and they were in the thick of the eddies, and the thundering breakers hammered the boat with titanic force. They were over more than half the channel now. A few more pulls meant land and safety.

"Pull, boys; pull for your lives!"

They did so, but there was a monster breaker chasing them like a wild beast after its prey. With lips set, the man in the stern concentrated every muscle upon the work: but, just as he seemed to be getting ready to beach the boat and clasp his wife in his arms, his hand relaxed, and he fell.

As Tom jumped to the oar, the big breaker took the boat and tossed her near enough in for the captain and the men, who were waist-deep in the surf, to grab her side. There was a turbulence of whirling water, of rapid movement, of strange words and anxious cries, and the boat and her crew and her passengers were safe on the beach.

All safe save one. His unconscious form rested listlessly on the boat's bottom. The men bore it tenderly to a place where the women had spread their shawls. The big captain knelt in the snow and tried to bring life from death.

"He must be taken home," said Tom. "We'll do it, captain. Your wrist is broken."

"Wrist be d——!" and the rugged old fellow lifted him in his big arms and carried him through the storm, followed by the woman who had asked God to keep him.

III.

"LIKE everything else, this marrying business is pretty much a matter of circumstances," explained the captain to me two years later.

We had arrived on the island after a long absence. The old fellow was changed — greatly changed. . His beard and his speech and his dress were all better trimmed, and he bore an air of intense respectability.

"Now, for instance," he went on, "take a man who 's got his notions set. He goes on through life without finding anybody to fit them notions. You can't blame him for staying single. But suppose that a man is put on a island, and he finds a woman there, — a fine woman, too, — and the circumstances throw them at each other every day in the week, why, what 's to be done, notions or no notions, but to call in the first preacher that comes along?"

"Captain, your logic is beneath respect, and, what 's more, I 'd like to know if an old woman-hater like you has any right to talk about marriage? Has an infidel a right to preach from a pulpit?"

"Yes, he has — when he 's converted. Have n't you heard?"

"You don't mean to say —"

"Yes, I do. I 'm converted. Oh, I 'm married. You need n't laugh. It was n't my fault; it was circumstances. You see, after Henry's death from heart-disease in that wreck, we all said the widder should have the school back; but there was another widder in the way, and she said she was going to stay on the island on account of her health, and there we were. Talk about your circumstances, two widders is a whole boatload. Well, I had to go to see the second widder about the school and so on, and I found out she was n't going to budge, and the only way to get her out of the school was for somebody to marry her. I swore to myself that Henry's wife should get back in that school, if I had to turn Mormon, and marry a whole county full of widders. So I kept on going to see her, and pretty soon we dropped school, and began to talk about other things, and so on, and such like, all of which was a d—d—draggled — "

"'Draggled,' captain?"

The captain gave a sigh of infinite pathos, and continued: "Yes, draggled! That's one of the drawbacks of marriage — she won't let me swear; won't let me say anything worse than draggled. Now don't you listen to the yarns the boys 'll tell you about the hard time I had giving it up. It was hard; but, as I was saying, that going to see the widder got to be a draggled sight pleasanter than I ever imagined, and inside of a month we called in a preacher. And so Henry's widder got the school, and she 's got it yet; and we built her that new house over yonder; and if there 's anything she wants on this island or anywhere else, the boys will get it for her, and thank her for letting 'em do it."

"I suppose, captain, that you like married life?"

"Like it? Young man, I was here on earth fifty-one years, and when I was fifty-two — the day the preacher came in — I commenced to live. I 've got the best wife in the world. She 's the best woman in the world except Henry's widder, who is the best woman in the world except my wife. But here we are at the station. You 'll stay for dinner, and after we eat, we 'll go over and look at the boy's grave."

It was delightful to be welcomed by such a woman as Mrs. Graves, but it was strange, very strange, to see the captain bow his head with real reverence, and hear him say grace with genuine unction.

Late in the afternoon we strolled over to the little cemetery. We stood together by the carefully kept grave, and read this inscription: —

Here Lies the Body of Henry Dane,

Aged 25 Years.

Who Gave His Life, November 19, for the Six Souls on the Wrecked Schooner Ocean View.

He Was a Hero and a Christian.

Erected by his Comrades of the Robb's Island Station.

"Greater love hath no man than this, that a man lay down his life for his friends."

TWO BOOMS.

SALEM City was booming. It was no ordinary boom; it was a flood-tide of speculation. Twice before it had risen above the tedium of its sluggish life, — once when the steamboats came, and once when the prairie caravans used it as a stopping-place; but the steamboats forsook its muddy banks and the caravans found a better road, and the village resumed its stagnancy.

But one bright day a nervous man, dressed carefully in a Prince Albert coat and a high hat, broke upon the monotony of the place. A dozen surmises were made as to his calling. A drummer he was not, for he sold no goods; a minister he could not be, for he patronized the bar: a lawyer he might be, but he declined to satisfy curiosity. He walked over the village; he talked of the climate; he asked questions until he exhausted all sources of information. In a day he knew who owned property, and the next day he had bought options on two squares, five business lots, and three outlying fields, besides purchasing outright the best house in the place.

Then he went away. He travelled four hundred miles until he reached a small city. He entered a modest house, and was promptly embraced by a sweet-faced woman, who called him husband, and by a brown-eyed girl, who greeted him with, "Well, Pop, are we going to move?"

Anthony Hoddle was a dealer in groceries. In a busy career of twenty years he had built up a successful trade, and his bank account had reached twenty thousand dollars. He was in the prime of life, a few weeks past forty, and his ambitions had long looked beyond their retail limitations. He felt that his ability was worthy of a higher destiny than the slow accumulation of fractional profits upon sugar and coffee and flour and salt mackerel. This ability was certainly better fitted for public display than for the comparative privacy of the store-room. It was the ability of speech that monopolized and overwhelmed by its natural volubility, a torrent of words and phrases that flowed with as much force, but without as much disorder, as a torrent usually does.

He was a natural talker, a personified organ of speech. He could tell the news of the week while he was dealing out a pound of coffee. He once disposed of the doctrine of eternal punishment before he filled his minister's order for four pounds of sugar. The incident is on record that he discussed the whole tariff question while he was getting a gallon of molasses. It is true that the day was cold and the molasses ran slowly through the spigot, but that does not detract from the glory of his performance. To use the words of one of the customers, he could talk an ebb-tide out, and still be in a condition to talk it back to a flood.

Mr. Hoddle's opportunity came when he heard that a new railroad was to be built with a place called Salem as its terminus.

"Yes, we 're going to move," he replied to the young lady's question, and when there were signs of sadness, if not of absolute disappointment, in the faces of the two women before him, he immediately rose to the occasion, and used his eloquence as if it was the crisis of his life.

"Of course it 's hard to break away from a place to which you are tied by twenty years of hard work, but it 's either that or the grocery business as long as the good

Lord lets us live. And I tell you now that I want a change, and so do you. I 'm tired of this humdrum, get-up-at-six-o'clock-in-the-morning-and-slave-all-day life, and so are you. Just at present Salem is not the loveliest place I ever saw, but it 's going to be a big city. In six months it will be crowded; in a year it will not know itself; in two years it will have a society, and as first settlers you will be aristocrats. We shall become wealthy, famous, happy. I 'm determined. I sell out to-morrow if I can. Next week we move."

The night, practically consumed in discussion, ended in a lot of new hopes undimmed by fears.

By the time they reached Salem a few other real estate speculators had learned of the railroad, and had descended upon the village. With these Mr. Hoddle made prompt acquaintance. He even sold them some land, — at twice what he paid for it, — and as quickly as possible he bought other ground on the outskirts of the town.

The boom began. It attracted strangers; it brought a horde of real estate agents; it revolutionized the village. The rough inn became a hotel; the eating-house outgrew its home-made name and paraded as a restaurant. Salem was no longer a village; it was Salem City. Hoddle's early arrival on the field had given him the prestige of a discoverer. He used it to its fullest value. He had the American genius of adaptability, and he ensconced himself snugly in the boom.

It was he who called the real estate men together for a consultation. They answered the summons. Interested in selfish results, their very selfishness made them anxious for the future of the town. They talked and advised and orated and discussed. But the speech of the day was made by Hoddle.

"Gentlemen," he said, "we all want this town to boom. How shall we do it? Two words solve the problem: stand together! We shall have our differences, our quarrels, and our contentions; but on one point we must be unanimous: we must talk this town up. If one of us goes away he must boom Salem City. Every man must be an advertising committee. Get interviewed in the papers; write letters; send out circulars; get the eye of the world on Salem; picture it as the fairest spot on earth. If any man says anything against our boom, denounce him as a traitor and a slanderer. Blow hard, and blow all the time. A boom is like a balloon; you 've got to inflate it. We may have our little differences and rivalries among ourselves — that 's all right; but one thing we must all do: we must give this boom a plenty of wind."

Before Hoddle could part the tails of his Prince Albert coat and sit down, a great chorus of approval greeted his outburst of practical eloquence. He had struck the key-note, and the choir of real estate speculators at once began an unceasing pæan to the glory of Salem City's matchless resources and immeasurable future.

Hoddle rode triumphantly on the crest of the boom. The admiring populace promoted him to a colonelcy, and Colonel Hoddle took hold of things with a fine grasp. He ran real estate speculation at full speed with both throttles open. Selling sugar at cost with three profits on coffee was n't a circumstance. When an investor drifted his way he gorged him with adjectives, deluged him with descriptions, and intoxicated him with figures. It was worth going across the continent to see him talk. His Prince Albert coat, as if afraid to conceal such a personality, flopped open and displayed a wealth of shirt bosom that seemed to reflect the lustre of his radiant optimism. He did not converse; he orated. His voice had caught the breeziness of the landscape, and no man who came in contact with him could escape without feeling that Salem City was destined to outgrow the fullest resources of the dictionary and the multiplication-table. If by accident any man doubted after Colonel Hoddle's shower-bath of statistical enthusiasm, the colonel would remark: "You see that square over there? Well, I bought it two months ago for two thousand. You can have it now for fifty thousand. Come back this time next year, and I 'll charge you a hundred thousand."

And so the boom developed. Organized exaggeration spread its fame. From one end of the country to the other the papers told of its marvellous growth. Investors who would demand abundant collateral and ten per cent at home, bought corner lots a half-mile from Salem's limits with no assurance except the flattering promises of the agents.

All this was intensified by the survey of the new Prairie and Deep Water Railroad, which was brought to the northern edge of the city. There it was hesitating as to which route to take to get it to the river-front. Colonel Hoodle had anticipated it.

"Gentlemen," said he, to a party of property owners whom he had assembled in his office, "this road is being built by New York capitalists. They 've got a plenty of money. They expect to spend it. The situation is in our hands. We can offer them free ground a part of the way and charge them like the deuce for the rest. What do you say to a syndicate?"

It was a fruitful suggestion. The syndicate was formed. The plan was to give the road right of way along the eastern side of Salem City, and make up all gifts a dozen times over by charging ten prices for terminal facilities.

From the company came a cordial letter thanking the citizens for their liberality. The offer would be considered and an answer returned. But as the days passed and no reply was received, Hoddle grew uneasy.

"Windsor, what do you think of it?" asked Colonel Hoddle.

Windsor had been in town only a week, — he came there, he said, on account of the climate, — but in that short time he had made the acquaintance of every man in the place, of Hoddle especially. "I like you, colonel," he had said, "because you are candid, and are a gentleman a man can trust." The colonel felt flattered and reciprocated the friendship. Moreover, he had seen that Windsor was a man of insinuating usefulness. He had a peculiar faculty for finding out things. For instance, the day before, a little information through Windsor had led to a bargain which netted him over a thousand dollars. Windsor seemed to be sincerely attached to him from the outset, and the colonel saw in him a friend who could be used. The abnormal circumstances of the boom made all sorts of attachments, and a day was as a week as far as social acquaintance went.

So the colonel called Windsor in to talk about the mysterious silence of the new railroad people. "It looks as if they were going to play some dodge on us and escape our syndicate," said he.

Windsor was silent. He was wrapped in corrugated thought. Suddenly he arose from his chair and walked up and down the office floor. Just as suddenly he stopped in front of the colonel, and exclaimed, —

"By George! I wonder if it is true?"

"What?"

"Why, this. Last night I took a stroll in the West End. I 'm troubled with insomnia, you know, and I often go out at night to walk myself tired, so that I can sleep. It was late. Near the county road I heard several men measuring with chains. What did it mean? I wonder if it was n't a surveying party?"

The colonel jumped up. "You 've hit it, my dear fellow — you 've hit it. My suspicions are correct. They 're trying to get an entrance by the west side."

"Not so fast, colonel; I may be mistaken. Let 's make sure of this thing. Come with me to-night, and we 'll see if the performance is repeated."

Late that night two men crept softly along the county road. At first they heard nothing, but presently sounds of a company of men drifted over the field. They crept closer. They saw chains and compasses. It was a surveying party.

The next day the colonel was a busy man. First he shifted a lot of his own real estate; then he kindly informed the syndicate of his discoveries. There was a rush to the West End property, and it was intensified upon the receipt of a letter from the company politely declining the proffers of the syndicate. Colonel Hoddle was happy, for he had four hours' start of all his fellow-agents.

In all the hurry of speculation Colonel Hoddle's family duties were not neglected. He had a happy household. Mrs. Hoddle was a kindly wòman, devoted, domestic, and popular. She had easily taken her position at the head of the new society of Salem City. Her daughter, Miss Elizabeth, was by common consent the belle of the future metropolis. She was a good musician, an easy-mannered, approachable girl who made friends and maintained her own independence. The family, probably the wealthiest in the place, had the handsomest house, and entertained freely. At the table the colonel was a royal host. After he parted the tails of his Prince Albert coat and sat down, there was not a dull moment.

"I tell you that Windsor is a perfect mascot," he said, the day after his West End deals. "If he will only stay in this town we will soon be millionaires, and I suppose I will be obliged to get elected to the United States Senate."

Windsor was invited to dinner. He made himself agreeable, and he and the colonel cemented their friendship by an entire evening of confidential conversation, sanctified by the plenteous incense of tobacco smoke.

A week later the colonel came home to

dinner in very good spirits. He parted the tails of his Prince Albert coat and sat down with his usual dignity. Something seemed to be amusing him. It got into his throat, and broke out into short spasms.

"What is the matter with you?" asked Mrs. Hoddle.

"Oh, nothing, nothing. I merely want to die — that 's all."

"What?"

"Oh, you ought to have met him, — J. Maximilian Ross. Dwell on the name, — J. Maximilian Ross. He wears it all, and he lives. He 's got it engraved on cards. He struggles under a stove-pipe hat. I 've seen him, and I want to go away — far, far away — far to a foreign shore."

"Anthony," said Mrs. Hoddle, severely, "are you intoxicated?"

"I don't know, Susanna — I don't know. Perhaps I am. J. Maximilian Ross!"

"In Heaven's name, Mr. Hoddle, who are you talking about? Be sensible for once in your life."

"Impossible, dear — impossible. Family association, you know."

At this point Miss Elizabeth came to her mother's assistance. It was the combined curiosity of two women against one man.

The great speculator met the onslaught by an ignominious surrender.

"Well," he said, "I 'll tell you. He came in this morning, young, fresh, and beautiful — more fresh than beautiful — fresh from the East, fresh from New York, fresh from a bandbox. But, thanks be to the fates, he was salted with money. That caught this bird; it always does. He wanted to invest. I undertook to give him a few facts."

"Facts?"

"No interruption, please. Yes, facts and figures. He opened his mouth and swallowed them, gulped them down, feasted on them. This afternoon he is to return, and perhaps I 'll buy you a case of diamonds on the proceeds."

"Where do I come in?" asked Miss Elizabeth.

"I 'll give you a father's blessing and J. Maximilian."

"Never mind the blessing," was the response; "I 'll take the man."

"My dear," said the fond father, "when the real estate agents of this great and booming city get through with J. Maximilian Ross he won't have enough money left to get back home. But" — looking at his watch — "here I 've spent all this time and not a sale to show for it. It's bad policy. Next time I get married I'm going to hunt up the ugliest woman in America. Then I'll never want to leave my business."

At supper that night he was as beaming as ever, and he had scarcely got the napkin tucked under his chin — which performance, I regret to say, the unperfected culture of the uncompleted city allowed — before he began to relate the events of the afternoon.

"J. Maximilian has invested," he said; "and what do you suppose he bought? That mudhole at the bend of the river. Cost me two hundred dollars. Sold it to him for two thousand: net profits, eighteen hundred. He's going to settle here, he thinks. Poor fellow! we'll try to make it pleasant for him, even if he does have to pay for it. I've invited him and Windsor to supper to-morrow. You'll have to stand him for an hour or so for my sake. There's nothing like flavoring business with a little hospitality, you know.

The next evening Mr. Ross came to tea. The ladies were anxious to see him. Their expectations were not disappointed. They saw a tall, fashionably dressed young man, rather good-looking, but entirely emotionless as far as outward indications went. He was not a fluent talker, but he selected his words with intelligence, and his occasional stuttering did not greatly interfere with his speech. The Hoddle family were talkers, and with Windsor's polite assistance they made up for ali deficiencies, and conversation went with a rush, breaking only when it ran against Mr. Ross's struggling syllables. The meal went off with comfortable and well-digested success, and the party adjourned to the parlor, where Miss Elizabeth made her first effort to engage the guest in conversation.

"I suppose you find this city very rough compared to your Eastern home?"

"Y-e-s," he said, slowly.

This was not an enthusiastic opening of the acquaintance, but it did not discourage Miss Elizabeth. She was of an impressionable age, men were few, and she admired fashion even on a dummy.

"It is a new town," she added.

"Y-e-s, but a mighty progressive one."

This was better. In fact it continued to improve, and it was not long before Miss Elizabeth and Mr. Ross were carrying on such a conversation that the colonel and Windsor begged permission to retire to the library for a smoke.

After a while Mr. Ross looked toward the

piano and asked Miss Elizabeth if she played. She did. Would she play? Certainly, and she did so with great satisfaction.

He was glancing over her music, and presently he held up a piece and said,—

"This is a very pretty song. Won't you sing it?"

"Look again," she replied; "it's a duet."

"Why, so it is! How stupid of me! But if you don't mind, I might spoil it by assisting you."

A cheerful assent, a few introductory bars, and two voices joined in the song. It was a good song well sung. Mrs. Hoddle sat silent, delighted with the music. But in the delight crept a fear.

"You have a lovely voice!" exclaimed Miss Elizabeth, just as the song was finished.

"Really that is not fair," rejoined J. Maximilian; "you took the words from me. You sing b-beautifully."

There were several more songs, and presently the colonel and Windsor returned from their cigars. The evening soon ended, and Mr. Ross and Mr. Windsor were invited to call again. These two men seemed perfect opposites—Windsor suave, effusive, confidential; Ross cold, distant, indifferent; and as they left the house they walked on as if each desired to be a stranger to the other.

"Well, what do you think of him?" asked the colonel. Miss Elizabeth had slipped away, and the colonel and his wife were alone.

"Anthony, do you remember the night you proposed to me?"

"Of course I do. We sang a duet, and you said I had a beautiful — yes, that 's the word — beautiful voice."

"People grow more truthful as they grow older."

But the colonel ignored the interruption. "It was the first time that anybody said I could sing at all, and I proposed on the spot."

"Anthony, after you and Mr. Windsor went to the library to-night, Elizabeth and Mr. Ross sang a duet."

"The mischief they did!"

"Yes; and they sang better than we did."

"Impossible!"

"And when two young people get to singing duets it 's serious."

"Well?"

"How would you like J. Maximilian Ross for a son-in-law?"

"Merciful Jupiter! Susanna, what do you

mean? Why, I 'd feel disgraced for life. I 'd sell out and emigrate."

The result of it all was that the colonel's antipathy to the young man increased a hundredfold. "If he was a man," he said, "I would n't mind. But that thing? Not much!"

In business he called him "the dude with the parted name." At home he alluded to him tenderly as J. Maxie.

"Colonel," said a caller one day, "I want to sell that lot of mine over in East Salem."

"Sorry, major," replied the colonel, "but I would n't take it at any price. The only person I know who 'll buy is that picturesque ass J. Maximilian Ross. You can sell him anything."

So it became the colonel's standing advice to people who wanted to dispose of unsalable lots to go to J. Maximilian Ross. They always went. They found the same indifferent young man. He did n't want to buy particularly; in fact he thought he had enough land already; but what was their price? That much? Oh, it was too high, you know. It was n't right to impose on a stranger. Then the owner would come down, and when he got low enough, J.

Maximilian Ross would offer a little less, and the bargain was closed.

More than a month elapsed. The boom was confined to West Side property, and the young city was full of speculation. J. Maximilian took life quietly. He visited the Hoddles; he took Miss Elizabeth driving; he made few acquaintances, and he wore the same indifference that he had brought with him from the East.

"Windsor," said the colonel, "it does seem that this whole town is palming off its bad lots on the dude, does n't it?"

"It looks that way."

"I notice that he is still sinking his money on the East Side. He was fool enough to buy that mud-hole. I wonder if I could n't get rid of those lots around it? Do you think we can work it?"

"Suppose I talk with him?"

"All right."

He did so. The result was a sale at a figure that made the colonel jubilant.

"Well," said he at the supper-table, "I 'm glad J. Maxie settled in this town. He 's such a tender bird, so innocent, so easy to pluck. I got several thousands more out of him to-day."

"I would n't boast of it if I were you," said Miss Elizabeth.

"My dear," responded the father, "if a fool and his money are soon parted, it 's the fault of the fool; and if nature did n't supply us with fools, what would become of speculation?"

"Father, did it ever strike you that Mr. Ross is not as big a fool as he looks?"

"No," answered the colonel, reflectively; "it strikes me he is a bigger fool than he looks."

All this did not affect the visits that J. Maximilian Ross made to the colonel's house,—visits which were musical with duets. Mr. Ross was very attentive, and Miss Elizabeth seemed bright and happy. The colonel bore it all with an easy grace. He believed in the fullest freedom, and he would do nothing to restrict the happiness of his daughter. Furthermore, he scarcely thought that anything would result from the acquaintanceship. He gave Miss Elizabeth credit for more sense.

But he calculated wrongly. It was the same old story. The director of those duets was a merry little fellow named Cupid. And he did his work well.

Mrs. Hoddle saw the result. "Elizabeth," said she, one day when they were alone, "has Mr. Ross proposed yet?"

"Not yet," was the reply, uttered in mock seriousness; "but I expect him to soon. He 's very slow, you know." And with a laugh to hide the rising blushes, she fled from the room.

Mrs. Hoddle shook her head and said nothing. She did not even mention it to the colonel.

But Mr. J. Maximilian Ross had something to say. It was about a week afterward. He entered the colonel's office, and found the great speculator alone. The colonel parted the tails of his Prince Albert coat as usual, sat down with dignity, and placing his fingers together, said: —

"Well, what can I do for you?"

J. Maximilian sat bolt-upright, and tugged away on his glove.

"Colonel, I came to ask a great favor of you."

"What is it?"

"The hand of your daughter."

"W-h-a-t? You?

"Yes; why not?"

"You?"

"If you wish any information about my position and my family — "

"Your family," interrupted the colonel, with steadily rising wrath — "your family?

Do you think my daughter wants to marry your family? How much will your ancestors honor your note for?"

"I have money."

"You have now. But, great Scott! how long will you have it? The way you're going, you'll be a beggar inside of six months. What do I care for your family? I've seen you; that's enough. I want my daughter to marry a man who can make money, not one who throws it away."

"Is that your answer?"

"Yes, sir, it is. And it will continue to be my answer until you can show that you have sense enough to get in when it rains. For Heaven's sake, young man, do something — do something! Try to be a man. Give nature some excuse for your existence."

"Is that all?" asked J. Maximilian, in the coolest possible way.

The colonel fell back in his chair. His feelings had overcome his powers of speech.

J. Maximilian arose, walked quietly to the door, and remarking, "Very sorry to have troubled you — good-afternoon," sauntered down the street as unconcernedly as if nothing had happened. The fires might have been raging within, but all was unimpassioned without.

Not so with the colonel. For a few minutes his collapse continued. Then he gradually recovered. The more he recovered, the higher his vehemence rose. He felt like the hero of Bitter Creek, who wanted all creation to come into that room so that he could get a chance to thrash it. It required two days for him to cool down to his normal temperature.

But the colonel knew womankind well enough not to adopt arbitrary measures. All he said to his daughter was: —

"Elizabeth, you are a girl of good sense, and I 've only one thing to ask of you. When you think of getting married don't marry a fool."

"I won't, father. Be sure of that."

J. Maximilian Ross continued to pursue a very quiet course. He had money, but he very frankly said that he could not afford to buy expensive property. He was willing to invest modestly, and wait for a gradual rise in values. The boom was going on almost entirely in West Side land. The contemplated railroad there promised to shift the business centre of the city and concentrate values in that locality. Westward the course of speculation took its way. The crowds went with it. On East Side lots prices fell.

As the only buyer, J. Maximilian Ross secured bargains at his own figure. He seemed to buy because the agents persuaded him into buying, not because he wanted it. One day he made an offer for the square owned by Colonel Hoddle. The colonel's price was fifty thousand dollars.

"Twenty-five is all I can give," said J. Maximilian.

"Then you won't get it," said the colonel.

The railroad people were strangely inactive. They had not begun operations around Salem. Suspicion took hold of the agents. As usual, the colonel consulted Windsor.

"What is the matter?" he asked.

Windsor pulled a letter from his pocket. It was from New York, and in it was this sentence: "We hear that the Prairie and Deep Water Railroad people have changed their programme. They are going to take their road to Concord instead of to Salem. They claim that it will be cheaper."

This perturbed the great speculator. He thought of it all night. The next morning he got the local paper from Concord.

"We can state on good authority," said the "Concord Civilizer," in leaded type, "that the new railroad has selected Concord for its terminus. This shows good sense.

Salem City — the idea of a one-horse town being called a city! — is nothing but a mud-hole worked by a gang of speculators who have sunk other people's money so deep that they will never see it again. Concord is the future metropolis! Hurrah for us! We will have ten thousand population inside of a year!"

II.

COLONEL Hoddle was a man of action. He did not hesitate. The boast of the "Concord Civilizer" by itself meant little. Taken in connection with Windsor's letter, it meant everything.

To Concord the colonel hastened. He looked over the town thoroughly; he found a large and active boom there. Prices had jumped, and he could buy nothing except a few stray lots, which he picked up with all eagerness. West of Concord was a tract two hundred acres in extent. Could he get that? He would try.

Back to Salem City he went. He told Windsor of the land, and asked him to find out who owned it. In a day's time Windsor got the information. He entered the office with a smile. "Who do you think owns that land?"

"I don't know."

"J. Maximilian Ross; and what's more, I believe you can get it away from him if you want it."

The colonel grabbed his hat, and without taking time to thank Windsor, made straight for Ross's office. He found the young man in. Negotiations for the purchase were begun at once.

"What will you take for it? Name your lowest price, and don't hesitate, for I have n't any time to lose."

"Well," replied J. Maximilian, with his usual slowness, "that land ought to be worth one hundred thousand; but I need some money, and I'll tell you what I'll do—give me that square you own on the East Side, that new house you have just finished on the Heights, and twenty thousand dollars in cash, and I'll deed you the two hundred acres."

The colonel rapidly computed the values. The square he held at fifty thousand, the house at ten thousand, and with the twenty thousand cash the total was eighty thousand. But the fall in the boom had knocked Salem prices down nearly one-third, and he was getting his bargain for something like sixty thousand.

"Young man," he said, "I 'll take it."

The papers were drawn up and signed that day. At tea the colonel was jubilant.

"I saw J. Maxie again to-day," he said.

"So did I," says Miss Elizabeth.

"But the case is different," replied the colonel, with a slight frown. "J. Maxie will soon be very sorry that he ever met me. There 's no use denying the fact that the boom in this town is played out; that railroad is not coming here. It 's going to Concord, and it will take the boom with it. Well, J. Maxie owned two hundred acres near that town of as pretty land as you could want. He does n't own it now; it is in the possession of your humble servant."

"How did you get it?" asked Mrs. Hoddle.

"Policy and cash, my dear, and my mascot Windsor. I expected to pay a hundred thousand for it; I got it for sixty. I was sorry that J. Maximilian was so easy to pluck, but forty thousand dollars is enough consolation to heal a week of sorrow. I got his land for twenty thousand cash, which I raised on mortgages, the East Side square that won't be worth twenty thousand one week from now, and that new house on the Heights."

"I thought you were going to give me that house some time for a wedding present," interrupted Miss Elizabeth.

"So I intended, my dear; but you know circumstances alter cases. After a while we'll move to Concord, and when you meet your fate there, I'll do the handsome thing and build you a palace. As for J. Maximilian, I suppose we'll have to leave him to pull his cash out of these Salem City mud-holes. Poor fellow, how unfortunate it is that nature did n't give him less style and more sense!"

For an hour the conversation lasted. It was an important subject, the probability of removal, but the colonel smoothed down all objections by describing the superior climate of Concord and the added riches that his new speculations would bring. They would live in a finer house, he would enter politics, and a trip to Europe should become a summer vacation. They adjourned to the parlor; a minute afterward J. Maximilian Ross was ushered in. Never was he so carefully dressed. Never did he appear so calm and so polite. He bowed with conventional courtliness, and then said, in his indifferent way, —

"Colonel, I came to see you about a little matter." .

"Business?"

"Not especially. I came to see if you would deliver the address on behalf of the city at the laying of the corner-stone of the new railroad."

"What city?" gasped the colonel.

"Why, Salem, of course."

"Young man, are you crazy? The railroad is not coming here; it is going to Concord."

J. Maximilian Ross raised his eyebrows in surprise. "I think you 're mistaken; it 's coming here."

"Explain yourself," commanded the colonel, with an excitement that was unusual to his nature.

The conversation had taken place so rapidly that the two men were still standing.

"When the plans of the new railroad were announced," said J. Maximilian, "everything seemed easy, but somebody got up a syndicate in Salem to make the company pay more for terminals than it could afford. So I was sent on here to see about it."

"You?"

"Yes. Of course you know that I am the representative of the company here?"

The colonel was speechless. Mrs. Hoddle looked on in open-mouthed wonder. Miss Elizabeth turned her chair to the fire and buried her face in her hands.

J. Maximilian talked on without the faintest sign of emotion. "I had a hard time," he continued, "to switch the speculation over to the western side of the city while I bought our right of way at reduced rates on the east; but it was a great success. We saved at least twenty thousand right down at the river front. I believe I bought that of you, colonel?"

The colonel groaned. "Go on," he said. "What about yesterday's deal?"

"Why, I had to have that square for the company's central building, and I could n't pay over twenty-five thousand for it. I tried to get it, but you would n't come down. So I put ten thousand in a lot of land at Concord, and got about eighty thousand for it. Sorry for you, colonel, but it had to be done."

"But Windsor told me that the railroad was going there!"

"I hope you don't trust Windsor; he is n't reliable."

The colonel's voice was growing husky. The color left his face. Suddenly he cried out, "Young man, you have ruined me!"

The cry did not disturb the young man's equanimity. He quietly replied, "Oh no, I have n't; I 've got until Saturday to keep the plans quiet. To-morrow will be Thursday. If you cannot turn that land over at a good profit in two days you 're not what I take you to be. But I make my silence conditional."

"What 's the condition?"

"That you deliver that address."

The colonel's smile returned. It cleared away the fog from his throat and the clouds from his face.

"Thank you, thank you," he said; "I will deliver the speech. I 'll make somebody pay me a hundred thousand for that property. But, Mr. Ross, if there is anything else in this county that you want, please let me know."

J. Maximilian looked over to the rocking-chair. Love's signal service worked to a charm. The colonel saw it; Mrs. Hoddle saw it. No words were needed to emphasize it. For fifteen seconds the air was eloquent with silence; it seemed like fifteen minutes.

"Perhaps you know now why I wanted

that house on the Heights. Elizabeth seems to like it so well."

"Yes," said Elizabeth; "father likes it too."

The colonel blushed — actually blushed; but presently he said: "I have only one favor to ask. Postpone this wedding long enough for me to pay my respects to Windsor."

"I don't think we can," said Mr. Ross.

"Why?"

"You see the climate does n't agree with Windsor as much as he thought. He 's afraid of a change. Sometimes people like him very much for a while, and then they turn around and dislike him equally as much. His midnight surveying parties will not be popular when people understand them. I fear, too, that he is responsible for that Concord boom, and when it reacts, as it will do next week, this locality will not be as healthy for him as he would like. All in all, I thought it best to send him back home."

"You?" demanded the colonel.

And J. Maximilian Ross looked up with all the innocence of a sudden surprise, and said, slowly and sweetly: "Really, this is singular. Did n't Windsor tell you that he was my confidential agent?"

The colonel looked at the young man in a dazed sort of way, and sank silently into the big plush chair. And for the first time in his life he forgot to part the tails of his Prince Albert coat.

As for J. Maximilian Ross, he walked over to Mrs. Hoddle, and unrolling a sheet of music, asked her if she objected to listening to a new duet.

IN THE EARLY CHRISTMAS MORNING.

WHEN Samuel Newton sat in his office the day before Christmas and looked vacantly out through the window, he was doing something he seldom did — he was wasting time. He simply could n't work. You can't expect a man to concentrate anything — even his mind — when he has proposed to a widow and is waiting for her to think it over. You can't expect a man to keep his energy moving when his mill property has been closed by a general strike, with no apparent likelihood of settlement. You can't expect a man to be satisfied with himself when he has outdone his own sense of generosity by purchasing a ten-dollar gift for a small boy, even if that boy be the widow's son. And when you combine the uncertainty of the widow with the certainty of the strike — not to mention the boy — what can you expect?

Well, anything! A bachelor in love after forty is a sight for the gods. The youth of twenty or thereabouts, or even the young man on the bright side of thirty, has the same emotions; but they fit him better. He nurses them as he does his mustache, and saves himself from absolute submission to the young lady by the somewhat cheerful conceit that he is a great fellow among the girls. But while love ceases to be an emotion and becomes a plan of campaign with many women after forty, with a man it engrosses — it overwhelms. It is the seething maelstrom in which the poor fellow is whirled around by alternate currents of ecstasy and despair. In fact, after forty love is a very serious disease, a kind of dizziness of the head and heart, and the condition of a patient who is waiting for a widow's answer is what the doctors call critical.

Rev. Paul Worthington said all this, and he ought to know, for he was in love himself; and he had a right to know about this particular case, which seemed to be the exception that proved the rule, because the young lady he loved was the cousin to the widow Samuel Newton loved. In the abstract, the Rev. Paul Worthington knew more about the art of love than Mr. Ovid who wrote the book, or the Massachusetts gentleman who married seventeen different wives in eight different States; but in the concrete he was a failure.

Incidentally, you would never have taken these two men for a pair of passion-tattered swains. Samuel Newton was the leading banker and broker of Sandfort's two thousand population, a prosaic, steady, uneventful sort of man, who had trained himself into a financial monotony. Rev. Paul Worthington, big of body and bigger still of heart, had charge of the largest church in town, and his earnestness, eloquence, and remarkable popularity had built its congregation to crowded proportions. He was the rare kind of clergyman who preaches the dogma of one denomination and practises the virtues of all. People shook him cordially by the hand and asked him to dinner. They bowed to Samuel Newton and passed on.

But the clergyman, with the vantage of the only intimate friendship in which Mr. Newton had ever indulged — they had been playmates and schoolmates and men together — knew that the broker possessed emotions and aspirations above the usual six per cent. For instance, when "Cash" contributed a good large sum to the church fund, and when the same anonymous benefactor helped the poor, the Rev. Paul Worthington, who distributed the money, knew who "Cash" was. The people did n't.

Mr. Newton was still staring into the void filled by the widow's uncertainty when the clergyman entered the office and said something about the false economy of people who preferred ruined carpets to the expense of a door-mat. The banker did not rise to the sarcasm of the occasion, nor did he properly greet the invitation which followed to go out on the sidewalk and indulge in a snow-battle.

"You 're talking nonsense," was his comment.

"My dear Samuel, nonsense is the wisdom of life. Without it existence would be a dirge; but with folly life is a song. Woe be to the man who outgrows the spirit of youth!"

There was no response.

"I think I said 'woe,'" he added.

The banker, ignoring both the original remark and the addition, arose and shut the door that led to the other office. Then, drawing his chair closer, he said with solemn and sudden confidence, —

"Paul, I have proposed to the Widow Stonington."

"How — how did you do it?" asked the astonished visitor.

"It was a premeditated act."

"Well?"

"I'll tell you all about it, but for Heaven's sake don't laugh at me. I thought that the strike down at the mill was bad enough, but this waiting for an answer is the most serious experience I ever passed through in all my life. I've been in love with her ever since we went to school together, but it was in my quiet way, and before I knew it she was engaged to Dick Stonington. Now she has been a widow four years, and you know as well as I do that I've been calling there off and on three years. Well, this week I determined to settle it; I've had enough of living alone. So last night I went to see her. I entered the room as usual; she took the little rocker by the lamp-stand as usual; I sat down in the big arm-chair over near the fireplace as usual. I thought I'd out with it at once, but it would n't come. So I talked about the weather; we talked about the weather; we got to talking about the town and by and by we were discussing your sermon of last Sunday, and when she indorsed what you said about the strength of human love, saving the world from absolute loneliness, I grabbed hold of each arm of the chair, and sitting bolt upright, with every nerve in my body tingling like an electric current, I said, 'Margaret, will you be my wife?'"

"Go on, go on," exclaimed the clergyman, when Mr. Newton paused.

"Well, it seemed to transfix her. Her ball of zephyr rolled to the floor, and her fancy-work got demoralized. I sat there half scared to death and afraid to move. She was just about to speak when Tom — that confounded boy of hers — came in and interrupted us. He stayed so long, and all my feelings became so completely mixed, that I simply had to get out of the room. She followed me to the door and said she supposed she would consider it, and would let me know. I asked her if two days would be long enough. She said that it would."

Mr. Newton paused, and then added, as if it were a postscript, —

"By the way, after I reached the walk she called to me and asked if I had left my umbrella. I said no, and came on."

"You said no!" exclaimed the clergyman. "You are a disgrace to your sex. Somebody ought to take you down to the mill-pond and cut a hole in the ice and chuck you in."

"Now, what have I done?"

"Done? Why, that umbrella was a hint for you to go back and get her answer, and you walked off like — like —"

"I don't care if I did," interrupted the banker. "I believe in full deliberation, although," a pause, "this waiting is wearing. Any way," another pause, "I gave that boy of hers a ten-dollar sled this morning. It's pure extravagance, I know, but don't you think it will help me?"

"Samuel," said the clergyman, impressively, "what a widow wants is not deliberation or sleds, but sentiment."

"Well, how ought a man to propose?"

"A man ought to propose with his heart, and not with his intellect; with his soul, and not with his bank-account."

The insinuation nettled the banker. He said something like "Bosh!" and added: "If you know so much about it, why don't you discuss the question with Catherine Downham?"

"I'll answer you seriously, although you do not deserve it," he replied. "I'm afraid.

It 's worth living a life just to love such a woman, — just to hope that sometime she may return that love. I have tried to bring myself to a proposal, but what if she should say 'no'? Is n't the hope of a 'yes' better than the risk of a rejection? When uncertainty is bliss, is n't it folly to have the dream dispelled?"

"You need a guardian," commented the banker. "I thought you were a man of sense."

They finally argued each other into general dissatisfaction. The discussion might have lasted all day had not Mr. Worthington ended it.

"I dropped in to see you," he said, "on an altogether different matter, and I 'm glad I did. We both need a fresh experience, and I 've a plan that will do us good. I want you to come to my house at midnight. Come quietly, and don't let any one see you. Never mind about that," he added, rising and heading off all questions. "I 'll explain everything to-night."

Promptly at midnight Samuel Newton walked into the clergyman's study.

"On time, as usual," was the greeting he received. "Sit down there and write something for me on this card."

The banker took a seat as requested.

"Disguise your handwriting and write, 'With all the happiness of a Merry Christmas.'" He did so.

"If I 'm not trespassing," said Mr. Newton, "I 'd like to know what all this is about."

"Certainly. I have had to make a new plan of distributing our Christmas remembrances this year. You see, we have only two or three people in our congregation who are really in want, but there are a lot more who go to other churches who need food and the churches are not rich enough to do anything for them; so I 've decided to use your three hundred dollars in seeing that they are not forgotten."

"Good for you!" exclaimed the banker, with more enthusiasm than he usually showed. "Your heart is bigger than your creed, as it ought to be."

"And to do this," continued the clergyman, "you and I, with a big sleigh full of things and Bucephalus for a reindeer, are going to play Santa Claus."

"We are going to do what?" asked the astonished banker.

"Now you can't back out. The town is fast asleep; the snow is deep; we 'll make no noise, and those unfortunates will wake up to-morrow morning to find Christmas dinners on their front doorsteps. How do you like it?"

"I don't like it at all. It's simply idiotic. Suppose we should be found out?"

"But we won't;" and the clergyman proceeded to prove with convincing earnestness not only that discovery was improbable, but also that it was Mr. Newton's Christian duty to go.

And then they got to talking about their boyhood days, — about a certain Christmas Eve, twenty-five years before, when the youths of the town, led by two particularly mischievous sinners, played sad tricks upon the innocent inhabitants; about the changes that had taken place, and the strange coincidence that had brought to the church as its rector the man who, as a boy, had rung the bell on that wintry night. They became reminiscent and — well, you know that men are only boys of an older growth — and the silence and the snow and the novelty of it all brought back in living distinctness the recollections of those days, and pretty soon the two bachelors were as young and as frisky as they had been a quarter of a century before.

At any rate, when one o'clock came the sleigh emerged noiselessly from the clergyman's gate. The town was as quiet as the night itself. No sound of revelry compromised its respectability. The clear stars which looked brightly down saw nothing but the universal whiteness of the streets and the house-tops, and the two muffled creatures snugly ensconced in a loaded sleigh.

The clergyman drove. He reined to the right and they were at once on their way to the lower part of the town, where the working-people lived.

"What a glorious night!" he said. "How eloquent is the stillness, — the stillness of sleep that knits up the ravelled edge of care; the precious oblivion that comes to the two thousand souls in this town, and buries their sufferings and their sorrows in eight hours of priceless peace."

"That is very pretty," whispered Mr. Newton in return, "but I 'd like to know where you 're going."

"We are on our way to the houses of the strikers, down near the mill," replied the clergyman.

"What!" exclaimed Mr. Newton, "those people? You know that those men have stopped our work and shut down our business, and do you mean to tell me that you are spending my money to help them out, to —"

"Yes, I know all about it," he interrupted. "We need n't discuss the strike here, but twelve of those men have families, and those families have nothing for a Christmas dinner. Back there in the sleigh are twelve baskets, and those women and children are not going hungry to-morrow if we can help it."

"But —"

"There are no buts about it. This is Christmas. The strikers may be wrong, but they have nothing; you capitalists may be right, but you have more than you need; aud all the right is never on one side. Suppose you had to discuss the matter on an empty stomach; would you feel merciful and charitable then?"

"Right is right," interrupted Mr. Newton.

"And there is no higher right than the right of man to expect humane consideration from his fellow-man, — the right of duty and the right of charity. But here is one of the houses. Samuel, you must do a generous act by getting out and putting one of these baskets on the front doorstep."

Samuel was backward about it, as a man naturally would be in his position; but after rapidly discussing the situation he agreed to do his part, only on the condition that he should not get out where there were any dogs; for if there was anything he feared worse than death itself, it was a dog.

With this agreement, the work began and progressed with signal success. Mr. Newton did his part, and as house after house was visited, and his thoughts of the good that might be done cheered and warmed his heart, he almost forgot the grief of lost dividends and became a Santa Claus in real earnest.

From these houses they went to another part of the town. There was in the air an exhilaration that had its full effect, and both men seemed to grow younger and livelier than they had been in twenty years. They cracked jokes in whispers, sang snatches of songs very softly, and once or twice made Bucephalus speed along under the mild suggestion of a whip.

Finally they made their way to the hills that overlooked the town. At the top was a street which ended at the gate, and this gate led to a house occupied by the family of Miss Catherine Downham. It was a large residence, far back from the street, at the rear of a long yard, and it was indescribably picturesque and beautiful amid the snow and quiet of the early Christmas morning. Next to it was another house, almost a counterpart in size and architecture. In fact, Samuel Newton's father had built both houses, and one of them he had sold to Mr. Downham. The other had been occupied by the banker until about three months previously, when, tiring of the loneliness, he had moved to quarters downtown.

"Now, Samuel," said the clergyman, "I'm going to ask a very great favor of you. I want you to take that basket back there and put it on the Downham porch. You can do it by going up your own lane and reaching over the fence. Of course no one will see you, but if you should be seen you'll be on your own premises, and nobody can say anything; and if anything is said about the flowers I'll own up to them. I got out at all the dog-places; the Downhams don't keep a dog, and you will be entirely safe. Now, please do this, Samuel, while I go down to the next street, where I will leave the last package. Then we'll be through and we'll go home."

Samuel at first objected, but gradually weakened, and finally consented.

He made his way to the gate at the top of the hill. He looked down the long stretch of snow-covered street, gazed for a moment at the two big houses, then carefully lifted the latch, opened the gate, and crept like a burglar toward his own house. When he reached it, after what seemed to him a longer time than he had ever taken before, he leaned over the fence and deposited the basket on the Downham porch. Relieved of his burden of fear he turned to retrace his steps. He had gone perhaps twenty yards, and was congratulating himself on his escape, when something happened. A big dog, with a bark that sounded like the roar of a lion, sprang forth from the shadows of the Downham yard, and with one leap cleared the fence that separated the two properties. For a moment Mr. Newton was paralyzed with fright, but an instant afterward his presence of mind returned.

The tactics he adopted would have done credit to an Indian fighter. He got over the fence into the Downham yard. The dog followed. Thus it became a contest of fence-jumping between the man and the animal. But as he neared the gate he appreciated the necessity of getting out of that neighborhood. If discovered, his character would be lost. So, resolving suddenly, as all great men in emergencies do, he darted like a frightened deer to the street, the dog following in noisy earnestness.

There is sometimes innate depravity in inanimate things, and the results of circumstances are beyond human providence. For instance, the sled that Samuel Newton had given the widow's son, James Stonington, should have been anywhere else in the world than at the top of a steep, slippery hill, for collision with a respectable citizen at the immoral hour of 2 A.M. But through some unaccountable accident it was there, and when Mr. Samuel Newton, aged forty and chased by a savage animal, rushed pell-mell athwart its path there were calamitous consequences. He stumbled, and in his wildly desperate effort to catch an impossible equilibrium he found himself sprawled upon something that immediately began to move. Before he could roll off it was gliding swiftly along, and before he could think of what to do the first steep dip of the hill had given it such a momentum that the barking dog was left in the rear. The poor victim, seeing his escape from the beast, thought little of what was to happen, and clung tenaciously to the means of his deliverance.

Down he went, like an unchecked train on a steep grade, like a comet shooting through space, like a wild something flying from danger and not knowing how or where to stop.

The Rev. Paul Worthington, waiting a square below, saw the apparition as it flew by. He was sure that he recognized the figure. He called, but there was no answer. He turned to follow, and as he did so he heard a crash, and a moment afterward discovered that an obstacle in the street had sent the sled to pieces against a tree and had rolled its passenger into a convenient snow-bank. He ran as quickly as he could to the spot, but before he reached there the banker was on his feet.

"If you say one word," he almost hissed, as he gathered his demoralized overcoat about him, "we'll have a fight right here and now. Take me home!"

. . . .

And that was not all.

Thomas, the servant, had to rap three times the next morning before Mr. Newton answered. A little bundle and a note were handed to him.

"Mrs. Stonington's boy brought them," said Thomas.

Mr. Newton took the bundle and unwrapped it. Mystery of mysteries! It was the muffler which he had worn. With feverish haste he tore open the envelope and read the note. As he did so, his face looked like a battle-ground of emotions. He sat down; then he got up and walked the floor and whistled and frowned and looked worried, surprised, disappointed, and gratified in constantly varying succession. Finally he remembered that he was standing in a cold room without slippers or dressing-gown to protect him from the pneumonia. He hurried to get both, and in putting them on recalled the fact that he had a stiff neck and a lot of sore muscles.

"There 's no fool like an old fool," he muttered, and then added, as if in reckless gratification, "but I don't care."

Mr. Newton could move quickly when he wanted to, and that Christmas morning, in spite of his muscular stiffness, he was an active man. Five minutes after he had eaten his toast and drunk his tea he was busily at work, and Thomas was hurrying down the street on important missions. Within a half-hour the servant returned, and was again sent forth, this time bearing a large bundle and pulling a sled.

An hour later the Rev. Paul Worthington walked in.

"How is Santa Claus this morning?" was his greeting, "and how are the dears and all the little reindeers?"

The banker looked at him solemnly and responded: —

"Did it ever strike you that two can play at the same game?"

"It is a poor game when they cannot."

"Well, this morning you have sent the best bunch of roses to Catherine Downham that the hot-house around the corner could furnish."

"I?"

"Yes, you; and on your card, on the one you left here — really, you should not leave your cards around so — is this inscription: 'Not words but flowers shall express my thoughts for you on this most blessed day.' I found it in a novel."

"I don't understand."

"Read this. Her son Jimmy brought it this morning."

The clergyman took the letter and read as follows: —

CHRISTMAS MORNING.

DEAREST SAMUEL, — I cannot tell you how delighted I was to find the flowers you left on the porch last night, "with all the happiness of a Merry Christmas." Do you know, Samuel, why I hesitated to answer you the other evening? I — pardon the suspicion — I was afraid that you had crushed all sentiment out of your life, and to me life without sentiment would be a world without sunshine. But this morning, when I received your remembrance, I was made happier than words can describe. You must come to dinner to-day, to receive my answer. And you must also tell me how you discovered that I was spending the night with Catherine Downham. I thought I recognized your handwriting on the card, even though it was somewhat disguised, but I was not sure of it until James brought in your scarf, which he found out in the yard, and which I return with this. I hope that the dog did not annoy you. James forgot to fasten it up last night. It was so romantic. With the fullest love,

Your

MARGERY.

The clergyman kept passing his hand over his forehead as if trying to solve it all.

"It's really extraordinary," he said. "I didn't know she was there — honestly, I did n't. Those flowers were for Miss Downham — you know they were. I got you to write the card so as to tease her about it — seriously, I did. But what 's done is done, and I congratulate you." Then, looking at the note again, he read, "'Sentiment'! 'dog'! 'dinner'! 'romance'! Superb, is n't it, Samuel?"

"Very fine," replied the banker, "but there has got to be another engagement before Christmas is passed. After you get through your morning sermon you had just as well go around to see Catherine and do your duty like a man. The flowers are there by this time, and if you try to deny them I 'll break a Commandment and compromise your standing in this community. You are not going to keep her single all her life, just to get her money for the heathen — not while I am her cousin-in-law elect."

Rev. Paul Worthington had to hurry off to church. As he stood in the pulpit that Christmas morning he scarcely knew his surroundings. All he saw was a young woman, "divinely tall and most divinely fair," with a delicate suffusing blush that seemed to reflect the soft and glorious beauty of a large bunch of roses which she wore. Lovelier than ever she sat in the corner of the pew, apparently as oblivious to the small congregation as the preacher himself.

How he struggled through the sermon he never knew. What he said he never remembered. But the events after the service will be as fresh to his dying day as the recollection of the bishop, who officiated at a double wedding which crowded the church to overflowing and reclaimed two bachelors from the evil of their ways.

Months afterward, when these two friends sat talking it all over, they were solemn and philosophical. Man's wisdom is largely man's conceit, and his success in love or in business adds to both.

"A good deed," said the clergyman, "is the best investment a person can make; it always pays dividends. Remember how easily a strike was settled after those Christmas dinners, and how smoothly you have gotten along since the new year began."

"And a foolish deed," said the banker, "keeps coming back like a counterfeit coin. I suppose I shall have to buy ten-dollar sleds every winter; but, thank heaven! Jimmy has given up the dog!"

THE COLONEL'S CALL.

"WALK right in, Colonel. I am very glad to see you."

"Suppose you close the door, Pendle. I want to speak with you privately."

Pendle stepped briskly to the door and closed it. His few steps showed a swift physical movement altogether at variance with the serene composure of his countenance. If asked to compare him with any other member of the animal kingdom, you would have at once suggested the panther; but a moment afterward you would have said, "the panther — and something more." His face was smooth, firm, immobile; but there was a nervousness in the eyes that seemed to be trying to see things out of the corners, and added to a certain air of expectancy that the panther has, there was a certain ambitiousness with it all that the panther has n't. You would n't have trusted him very far, and you would n't have liked him very much; but you would have had more respect for his personality than to have classed him with the usual mediocrities who are in practical politics.

The other man was older and altogether different. He walked with the aid of a cane, and his solid manly shoulders and erect head looked military. He was tall, handsome, and grave, and his face was of the square honest kind, with eyes that seemed to reflect a rugged old soul that had known the world without having been soiled by any of its meanness. His voice fitted his appearance. It was a conclusive voice, and it sent its words straight to its mark.

There was nothing in the office to distinguish it, except, perhaps, a certain feeling that the furniture was standing around in a way that made it appear that it was not altogether at home. There was a large desk, and behind this Pendle sat after his visitor had found a seat in the leather-covered office-chair.

"I am at your service," said the politician.

"I came to see you in reference to the election in our ward," said the older man. "Entirely against my wishes and commands, my boy" — the boy was thirty-five — "has accepted the nomination on the reform ticket. He did it from conscientious consideration of what he conceived to be his duty as a citizen, and I honor him for his scruples and regret his judgment. But, as he has taken the step, I want to see him succeed, and I have therefore come to see you on my own responsibility."

A suggestion of a smile ran around Pendle's mouth as he said, "I would like to aid you, Colonel, but you know I am on the other side of the fence."

The Colonel apparently did not notice the interruption, and went on: "You have placed against him on your ticket a man without any character whatever, one of these little scoundrels who rent out their souls for a few years of cheap notoriety, — a person whose vote belongs to you, and who is, therefore, of importance to you personally."

With all his coolness, Pendle flushed. He was about to speak, but the Colonel continued, —

"There are enough respectable votes in that ward to elect my son, — enough will be cast to elect him; and the only way to defeat him is in the manner which you understand better than I can tell you. Now my visit here is to inform you that if you attempt any business of this sort, I shall be put to the trouble of demanding a settlement."

Pendle took up a paper-knife and tapped it a moment in his open hand. Then he spoke, his flush having given way to paleness. "Colonel Hall," he said, "passing over the indelicacy of your action in coming to this office and speaking as you have done, I wish you to know that this is a party matter, and not a personal matter. McGurke was regularly nominated by the party, and he will be supported by the resources of the party organization. The fact that I am at the head of that party organization, regularly placed there, I do not consider a dishonor, and I certainly shall not be recreant to the trust that has been confided in me."

"I did not come here to discuss evasions or organizations or glittering generalities; I came to talk to *you*." And the Colonel raised his finger, and slowly pointed it at Pendle as he emphasized the word. "I know you, perhaps, better than you know yourself. You have succeeded wonderfully well in this city, because you have ability — very great ability." Pendle bowed slightly, and the Colonel resumed: "Yes, very great ability, as a shrewd, exhaustless, persistent manipulator. I admire it in you, because it's your sole stock in trade."

"Colonel Hall," began Pendle.

"Sit still, Pendle, and let me do the talking. You will perhaps recall a few incidents from the past. If your memory is good, you will recollect that you hung around my command for awhile, and that your victories were confined exclusively to the commissary department. You were a coward then, and you are a coward now, and the only reason that you and your gang boss and rob this town as you do is that the people are bigger cowards than you are. Some day they will wake up to their duty, and will wonder why they stood you so long; but in the mean while you are piling up wealth that does not belong to you, and are getting the impression that you are invincible."

"Colonel Hall, I wish you to understand that I will not be insulted in my own office!" exclaimed the cool man, losing his coolness.

"It 's not insult, Pendle; it 's truth. For five hard years I did some fighting to help save the institutions which you are disgracing, and I have the right to speak my mind. I am not the sort of person to go into politics and make speeches and get cheated out of my rights, because I despise its tricks and its lies and its lowness. I prefer to deal with you direct, and that is why I came. You will, therefore, understand that if you send any of your gang of repeaters or bribers or scoundrels up in our ward to count in McGurke, you will be obliged to answer to me personally; and, old as I am, I will give you a thrashing that will make up not only for the present, but also for some of those derelictions of the sixties. That is all, Pendle, and I will say good-morning."

Pendle did not reply. The colonel arose and with head and shoulders erect marched out of the room. His big cane seemed to hit the floor with an increased force and he passed down the steps and on up the street with some of the same martial vigor of the days when he led his boys to the front of the fight.

Pendle had picked up a cigar which he failed to light and he chewed it more savagely than usual. Then he threw his head back and looked steadily at the ceiling. Finally he moved forward and tapped a bell. The clerk entered as quietly and as humbly as if in the presence of majesty itself.

"Go find Roster and tell him to come here at once. He 's probably at McCuddy's in the back part of the saloon."

Within twenty minutes Roster appeared.

"Sit down," said Pendle. "I have been looking over the city again, and I have decided to let Andy McGurke take care of himself. Save your crowd for the next ward to help Stine."

"But say," interrupted Roster, "if we don't give McGurke a boost he won't be in it."

"McGurke must look out for himself," said the boss, decisively. "We 've done enough for him already, and if he kicks we 'll see that the saloons he owns don't get licenses. But look here, Roster, keep all this mum until McGurke pays his assessment."

"All right," replied the heeler, meekly; "but it 's —— tough on Andy."

When he went out Pendle took a walk around the room. Finally he paused at a window, and as he looked out on the perfect October day he said, with something of a smile, —

"I am very much afraid that if there were more Colonel Halls in this town, there would be a great deal less of Pendle."

THE NOMINATION.

DAVID GAD and his good wife Ruth were sitting in the easy chairs resting after the day's work. He had closed the store at nine o'clock. It was a little cool for September and the windows were down. The light was turned low, for David and Ruth were economical, even in the matter of coal oil.

People said that David was a born success. They could not understand sometimes how it was so, because his father never had the gift, but they were not able to deny facts, which facts were that David was making money and was enjoying a solid reputation among his neighbors. When he started out most of them laughed at him; but the ones who laughed loudest now generally loafed the longest around his store. His marriage to Ruth Bland, daughter of old Jonathan Bland, helped him along.

Ruth was as practical in her ways as David, and such a useless expense of time and money as a wedding journey did not enter their thoughts. They went at once to their little home. David's old friend, John, was with them as clerk, and a very good one he was. Ten years went by and made David a rugged, substantial man. As he sat in the big rocker it was easy to see that he was a person of more than ordinary force. He was one of the Americans who succeed, a man of more mental activity than speech, a cautious, shrewd, far-seeing man,—at least this was Colonel Short's description, and he, being a politician, was a good judge of men or he would not have been a successful politician.

"David," said Ruth, "what is this talk about you and the sheriff's office?"

He looked up quickly and shifted his position before replying. "Where did you hear that nonsense?" he asked.

"All the folks are talking about it. I heard some men discussing it while you were out of the store to-day, and saying that Colonel Short had been to see you about it. The people seem to think you'll make a mighty good man for the place."

David smiled in a sober kind of way, and nursed his knees with his two hands. Presently he looked up, and said: "Ruth, a man of convictions should take an interest in politics for the good of the party which represents his principles, and not for any ambition which merely represents his own pride. I have voted the ticket and done some work for it, not with the hope of any office, but because my conscience and my judgment dictated that course. If people misconstrue my motives, it is very wrong."

"But, David, if they should give you the office — "

"Yes, if they should give me an office, what then? Four years of laziness, and afterward a return home to find our business all gone, or taken up by some one else. No, Ruth, you and I have had too hard a time building up this trade to have it ruined by politics. Let us keep on in our course, for we know not what a change might bring forth."

Ruth was silent for a while. The mention of the possible honor had aroused a quiet but unexpressed ambition for town life, had suggested the possibility of some of that change which every woman from Eve down has always secretly longed for. But David's practical words had brought out her common-sense, and shoved the ambition back into the closet of her heart. She closed the door upon it and sighed.

"I guess you 're right. You 'most always are. But who do you think they 'll take in your place?"

"I am for Major Powderdry," said David, with considerable emphasis.

Mrs. Gad was greatly astonished. "Major Powderdry!" she exclaimed. "Why, goodness gracious, David! he has n't done a thing in his life except to run for office and run into debt."

"That 's just it, Ruth. The good Lord has laid out for us certain duties in this world. A man may sometimes get away from his path, and wander over the field; but he always has a kind of an idea of what he is living for, and he is pretty apt to hit the road while he is tramping around. Now Major Powderdry's business is running for office. It don't pay much, but he sticks to it. Mine is running a store. I 've got along all right in the store, because the people have encouraged me. What the major wants is more encouragement. So let him have it, I say, and let us all elect him. Then, too — but of course you need n't mention it — if he gets through, he may pay us that little bill he owes us."

"Well, David, you certainly look at things with both eyes," said Ruth, with a decision that had in it a small undertone of admiration.

"Of course I do, Ruth, and when they fail to see what 's what, I know two other eyes that are mighty pert about finding the right side."

Ruth smiled, and felt quite happy. It was n't often that they paid compliments to each other.

"Ruth," said David, after a pause, "if the folks talk any more to you about me, just say that David is too busy attending to the store to go running across the whole county for an office, and that he votes the ticket for his convictions and not for rewards, and that he has said that Major Powderdry would make a good man for the place. Don't go out of your way to say this, but if anybody makes you talk, why, just put it to 'em straight and earnest like; if you want to, you might add something about your not caring for me to give up a good business for any such foolishness, and so forth and so forth."

Ruth said she would, and as ten o'clock had arrived, they locked up the house and went to bed. But before going to sleep David added, "And, Ruth, you might say that the talk Colonel Short and I had was on private business."

It did not require an age for anything to get over the district. News was scarce in Sussex.

Somebody had mentioned David Gad's name for the shrievalty. It met with favor. It was time the district was getting the office. David was a good party man, a reliable, conservative citizen, and a neighbor who was popular. The people talked quietly at first, but after it was known that David and Colonel Short had had a long talk, the discussion took a wider range. As it became more public it aroused a factional opposition, led by the voluble and oratorical Major Powderdry, a talkative upholder of party principles, and an inveterate seeker for a place on the ticket. David Gad said nothing, and attended to business.

The day after their little talk, Ruth left David at the store, and made a few visits. The matter of the office came up for discussion everywhere she went. She was not slow in making prompt and decidedly emphatic comments.

"Yes," said she, "I have heard that they are talking about David; but I reckon it's a lot of breath wasted. He's been a-working going on ten years building up his store, and he ain't such a goose as to throw away his business for an office. That talk he had with Colonel Short was about a private matter. There ain't much money in politics, and as for our part, we 'd rather have what we 've got than go to trying a change. David don't vote the ticket expecting to be paid for it; he 's not that kind. As far as I 'm concerned, I 'm glad of it, for it 's not everywhere you can get good neighbors. What 's more, David 's looked upon as a good man now, while if he was to go into politics, goodness only knows what they 'd say against him. And David ain't one that takes such things easy. He told me no later than last night that he was in favor of Major Powderdry. 'If our district is to have it,' said he, 'why, give it to Major Powderdry.'"

The good wives that good wife Ruth talked to in the afternoon told it to their good husbands at supper, and before bedtime it was generally known that David Gad was for Major Powderdry.

The major heard it at first with incredulity, and then with joy. He knew David Gad's endorsement would have great weight with the people. "I have always liked David," he said. "He is a man of business, a man of honor, and a credit to this neighborhood. I have watched him since he was a boy, and each year has increased my good opinion of him. When the people talked about his name I opposed it, because I knew that it would only bother him."

The major talked in this strain so as to ease his conscience and convince himself of what he never believed. That was a peculiarity of his oratory as well as of his conversation. He could talk himself into any belief, while the cold and listless crowd stood by and doubted.

The next day he dropped in at the crossroads store. He found Mr. Gad in an unemployed interval, and took possession of it with voluble but diplomatic promptness. He complimented the weather, the store and David, and asked, with solicitous earnestness, for the health of Mrs. Gad, and then plunged boldly into the purpose of his call.

"I hear," said he, lowering his voice, "that you have stated that you will endorse me for sheriff."

David took it in a matter-of-fact way, although he secretly enjoyed the major's polite circumlocution.

"Yes, major," he said, with business bluntness; "I 'm for you. You ought to have it. This district ought to have it. And the way for us to get it is to get it."

This roused the major's oratory. "Well said, Mr. Gad, nobly said. In the distribution of the legitimate rewards of the party, the just and equitable deserts of noble old Sussex have not been recognized. It will be a proud privilege for me to lead in the demand for this recognition, and I ask you, sir, that you will allow your name to be used on the delegation to the convention — as the head of that delegation, sir?"

The major said this with great personal applause, and David seemed very much impressed by it. But the merchant was doubtful. He rubbed his chin in a meditative way, and took some time to respond.

"Now, major, I want to keep out of politics."

"Do not say that, Mr. Gad. It is upon such men as you — upon the yeomanry of the party, if I may say so — that the selection of good standard-bearers and the perpetuity of free institutions must depend. You owe it to your district, sir, to be a member of that convention."

David paused again; he paused so long that the major walked back and forth uneasily.

"Well, since you put it in that way, of course I guess I 'll have to think about it," said the Sphynx at last. "But arrange it as quietly as you can."

A light of joy illuminated the face of Major Powderdry. He grasped Mr. Gad's hand and thanked him, not once, but countless times. Presently the emotional equilibrium was restored, and David announced that the next day he was going to start through the county on a business trip. He had the agency for a new machine, and he had been directed to place its sale in different stores of that territory. "I 'll see how things look in politics, and put in as many good words for you as I can."

The interview was brought to an end by the entrance of a family party in search of shoes and molasses. Major Powderdry went home with a happy heart. He was already beginning to enjoy the office and its perquisites — the perquisites mainly.

Mr. Gad's business trip occupied three days. He enjoyed it. Being well-known and well-esteemed, it was agreeable to meet people and talk with them. Besides, he sold more machines than he expected. When he arrived home the delegation had been agreed upon, and he had been placed at the head of it by the unanimous desire of his colleagues.

He reached the store just before twilight, and he had scarcely finished his supper before Major Hamilton Powderdry called. The major was more than anxious to hear the results of the journey.

"I am glad to see you back, Mr. Gad — very glad; and I hope you are the messenger of good news."

"Well, yes, major; I did remarkably well with the machines, — a great deal better than I expected."

"I congratulate you, sir — I congratulate you most sincerely. How did you find the political complexion? Was it favorable?"

"Oh, politics? Oh, yes! So I remember. Of course, major, I was mainly on business, but in the demands of that business I did not forget you. I did not forget our district."

The major rubbed his hands and smiled. "Thank you, Mr. Gad — thank you. What — what did you hear?"

"Well, I guess I better give you an itemized account, — a bill of particulars, so to speak."

The major was greatly pleased.

"First, I went to Forktown. I found that they are going to send a solid delegation down for Boggs. They were quite earnest about it; said that their district ought to have the nomination, and that Colonel Short had half promised it to them, and that they were going in to win. Of course it was n't much use to talk against such feeling as that, although I did tell them that in Major Powderdry, Sussex had a candidate that she was proud of."

"Thank you, Mr. Gad, thank you. We 'll soon down Boggs. Their talk about Short's support is nothing but a bluff. How about Bethel?"

"Well, Bethel 's got the fever too. They say they hain't had the sheriff for twenty years, and that they are going to pull for it this time, or break the traces. They 're putting up young Jones, and he 's working like a beaver. I slipped in a few words for you, major, but they brought up the argument that Sussex had it sixteen years ago, while it 's been twenty years since it went to Bethel."

The major uncrossed his legs, and nodded his head. "That 's all right," said he. "I know Jones. He 's active, but that 's all. We 'll circumvent him."

"From Bethel I went on down to Drawbridge and Forks. They are not far apart, you know. I found out that they had nobody in particular that they wanted, but Jones had sent down some missionaries and captured Drawbridge, and Boggs' men were at work at Forks. There is where I did some talking. I told them of our demands, of our candidate, of you, major, and your long service to the party. I said: 'Gentlemen, here is a fine man and an esteemed citizen, who has sacrificed time and effort in campaign work, who has fought in the front ranks, who has never flagged or proven recreant to his duty. He is the man we offer you, and we ask that you help us to nominate him.'"

"Thank you — thank you! Did you convince them of the wisdom of that course?"

"Not quite. They would n't commit themselves. So, to keep them from going to Boggs or Jones, I persuaded them to put up their own candidate. 'If it 's to be a grab game,' I said, 'why don't you take a hand?' Then I left, and went on down to the lower districts, where they don't care who gets the nomination, for the good and sufficient reason that they have had it for the last three times. However, I came back by Drawbridge and Forks to-day, and I found that they had put up their men, Hanson for Drawbridge and Withers for Forks."

The major's bright face seemed clouded. "Do you think," he asked, "that it was wise to bring two more men into the field? Won't it complicate matters?"

"Well, major, I'm a business man, and I look at it in a business way. I argued that if those two districts were disposed to go against us, the best way would be to make them fight each other as well as ourselves. It takes them away from Boggs and Jones. Now we have eight districts, and no nomination can be made until one of the five breaks to some other candidate. You stand well, major, and your genius must make a combination and win. You can do it, can't you?"

When the major saw it in that light he was radiant. "Why, David," he exclaimed, growing more familiar, "you are a Napoleon of politics. It's a great arrangement. I know Hanson and I know Withers. I'll see them; I'll deal with them; and when the convention opens, we'll give Boggs and Jones the biggest surprise party they ever saw."

This was Saturday. The convention met on the following Tuesday. The interval was fully employed. Everybody talked politics. The major led. He was exhaustless.

Hope beamed on his smiling countenance like sunshine on a morning-glory.

"Well, I never saw such a sight in all my born days," said Mrs. Gad. "The major acts as if he 'd been elected and got all the offices in the State."

"Yes," said David, "the major is enthusiastic. He has a sanguine temperament."

"He used to talk against you so. Now he 's praising you to the skies. There ain't any word too high or too big for you. It 's a strange thing, this politics."

"Very strange, — very strange," replied David, nodding his head. "It shows the changeableness of human nature, Ruth, the instability of character. If I had run for this office in an open way, as the folks wanted me to, the major would have been going around abusing me and getting up his movements against me, and I guess he 'd come near downing me. But now I am one of his delegates, and he is as sweet as a hogshead of molasses. How much better it is, Ruth, to have the friendship of everybody, even though we have to put ambition aside!"

The delegates from Sussex met at the cross-roads and started to town bright and early. David accepted his importance as the head member of the delegation modestly. Major Powderdry was gorgeous in a new high hat and an enlarged vocabulary.

"David," he said, with confidential earnestness, "you hold the delegates solid. I'm an old hand at this business, you know, and if you stick together while I do the work and pull the wires, we 'll win as sure as the sun will shine."

"That's it, major," he answered. "We 'll depend on you. I was never in a convention but twice before, you know, and both times they had the ticket made out, and all we had to do was to vote it through. This business is a little new to us, and I guess it 'll be a heap more exciting. Just let me say one word: don't let 'em bully you. Stick right up to it, and stay in the field as long as you can."

This warning aroused the major's latent pugnacity. "David," he said, "I 'm in this fight to win, and I 'll stay at the front till the battle is over and the cows come home."

So, with discussion and warning, and advice and suggestion the delegates proceeded. The temperature of their determination rose steadily, and by the time they reached town they were ready to march into the convention and demand the nomination for sheriff as the right of Sussex District.

But they ran into other determined bands. With the other four candidates in the field the situation was lively. The advocates of each man were importunate and vociferous. Into the arena the statesmen from Sussex, led by the intrepid Powderdry, advanced with argument and inquiry.

The Quantico County court-house, where the convention met, was a sombre building of brick, fronted by a large square. Outdoors and in-doors the groups were discussing and canvassing. Opposite the square was the law office of Colonel Short. To and from that place flowed steady streams of delegates. Colonel Short was the county leader — the "boss." Some came from his office in smiles, some in frowns, and some in doubt.

David was button-holing a man from a lower district when the major touched him on the shoulder.

"I 've been to see Short," whispered he, "I talked plainly to him, as a man with my strength should. I told him I had the united support of Sussex District, and that our district was entitled to the nomination. 'You 're probably right, major,' said he; 'but there are four other gentlemen from four other districts who say the same thing, and I don't see how we 're going to settle it except by fighting it out. Whoever wins, we 'll get a good sheriff, and I wish you luck!' Now, David, what is there in that? It looks stormy. Do you think we 'll get through?"

"Well, major, we 're doing all we can, and trusting to you to uphold the rights of our district."

The major's backbone stiffened, and he proceeded a second time to work. He saw everybody, made a hundred indefinite promises, and attempted every coalition that a man of twenty-five years of political failure could invent.

He was still at it when the hour for the assembling of the convention arrived. The delegates were in their seats, too much impressed by their importance to say much. The crowds struggled in and filled the benches of the court-room. A buzz of speculation and expectation arose to the ceiling and resounded between the walls. Occasionally a laugh interrupted the monotonous hum, or a pompous citizen came in, and talked loud enough to make himself heard above the noise.

A clapping of hands and a few thuds of heavy boots on the floor announced the approach of the chairman of the County

Committee. He mounted the rostrum, called the body to order, and said a few words which resulted in more clapping of hands and more boot thuds. With one or two soaring exploits in oratory, the election of the officers of the convention, the appointment of the committees, and the necessary preliminaries were arranged.

There was a recess for dinner. The interval was a time of heroic effort on the part of Major Powderdry and his competitors; but the more they worked the greater their doubt grew.

"David," whispered the major again, rather more agitated than before, "I 'm afraid it 's a case of every man standing pat, and staying in till the light goes out."

David did not exactly grasp the simile, but he told the major to remain firm.

The session opened. There were more speeches and more enthusiasm, and then the real work began. There was not much delay in the first nominations, but when the sheriff was reached a general movement seized the delegates and the on-lookers. They expected something worth seeing. But just as they got fixed for the excitement, a delegate arose and moved that the nomination for sheriff be postponed until the rest of the ticket was agreed upon. This caused a little fight, but it ended in the desired postponement.

In an hour's time the ticket was complete with the exception of the sheriff. That contest opened with great earnestness. For the purpose of saving time the nomination speeches were brief and formal.

The voting began. Five districts had their candidates. The three other districts distributed their votes with impartial favor. Ballot after ballot was cast without an approach to a result. The feeling became intensified. Two hours went by, and still there was no nomination. The districts were sticking to their men, and a nomination was impossible unless one of them broke. Supper-time drew near. Some delegates began to get hungry. All wanted to go home. But their earnestness triumphed over appetite. A new ballot disclosed no change. Major Powderdry's hopefulness was oozing out, but he was sticking like grim death. Suddenly some one whispered in his ear, "Major, Colonel Short wants to see you in the jury-room."

A great hope surged through the major's soul, and he tiptoed to the door, and in a minute was in the presence of the party dictator.

"Major," said the colonel, "what are you going to do?"

"Stick," he answered.

"Listen to me a minute. We 've got a good ticket, and we 've got a tough fight ahead. You five men in there are getting so hot against one another that not one of you can possibly win. You can't; they can't. Now, why not name the man?"

"Who?"

"Who is your choice?"

"David Gad would be a good man, but —"

"Well?"

"He won't take it."

"Get him out of the room, and give us time to nominate him, and he 'll have to take it."

The major saw the situation. He paused. He considered. He could not be nominated, — why not nominate? He could not be Edmond, — why not Warwick? Colonel Short argued. The major decided. He would do it. Rushing to the court-room he got David Gad and brought him to Short. Then telling him to stay there till called, he rushed back. Everybody left the jury-room to watch the convention, except Short and Gad. At the furthest window they whispered earnestly.

A new ballot was about to begin, when, at the request of Major Powderdry, one of Colonel Short's smartest lieutenants — young Carr — arose and asked permission to say a word. There was some grumbling, but a vociferous "Ay!" yielded him the privilege. He mounted the platform:

Mr. Chairman and Gentlemen, — We are going to win. (Applause.) We have got a good ticket. (Applause.) Harmony is thick and beautiful around here. (Smiles.) The only discordant note is a little difference of opinion about the sheriff. (Laughter.) We are burdened with five good men, — embarrassed with riches. My fellow delegates from this district and myself have voted for every one of them on the various ballots, and to save our lives we can't say which is the best man. (Applause and laughter.) We 'd like to nominate you all. (More laughter.) But it would be like putting too much sauce on the apple-dumpling; it would make the ticket too rich. (More laughter and applause.) Now I want to get home some time to-night. So do you. We want to leave with the knowledge that we have done our work. We don't want to carry away any hard feelings. It is for that purpose that I arise here on behalf of several districts, including our own, to suggest a name that will be endorsed by every man in this convention, by the whole county, that will add strength to the ticket and give enthusiasm to the party. I can pay this name no higher tribute than to say that it is the peer of the gentlemen who are now before this convention. (Applause.) In the interest of harmony, in the assurance of victory, and in the hope of getting my supper before breakfast, I nominate David Gad, of Sussex District."

The surprise was complete. The applause began slowly; then it took a jump; and finally it swept through the room and carried everything before it. It gained momentum when it was whispered around that David had been purposely gotten out of the room. Major Powderdry led in the enthusiasm. The nomination was quickly seconded. A ballot began. Before it was half taken, the nomination was made. A great howl went up.

In the jury-room Colonel Short looked at David and remarked, "It seems to be all right."

As David smiled in reply, the door was burst open, and in rushed Major Powderdry, his face beatified with unanimous joy, his arms in ecstatic gesture, his coat tails flying with nervous enthusiasm, and his whole being full of the bliss of victory — for his district.

He took David, dragged him before the convention, and shouted, "Hurrah for Sussex and our next sheriff!"

As the cheers went up, David asked what it all meant. He was the idealization of innocent astonishment. The delegates seemed to enjoy it.

And so did Colonel Short, who was standing in the jury-room door and looking smilingly on. He was thinking of the possible future in politics for a man of David Gad's tact and scheming.

It was late when Mr. Gad reached home, but Ruth was patiently waiting for him. The news dazed her, and he did the talking.

"Now don't say a word about it, my dear. It 's the best paying office in the county. The people think it 's been shoved on me. Let them think so. Colonel Short and I won't deny it. Oh yes; you were asking why I did n't tell you all about it. Well, my dear, running a store and running politics are two different things. If you want anything in the store, the best way to get it is to ask for it. If you want anything in politics, the best way to get it is to get it without asking for it. And moreover, my dear, a truthful woman like you is never safe in politics, unless she don't know what she is talking about."

THE OPENING GUN.

AT first David Gad's nomination for sheriff was received with great enthusiasm. All this made David's wife Ruth happy. Politics was n't such a bad thing, after all.

But gradually the enthusiasm began to cool. David's party opponents, seeing the necessity of finding some weakness in his candidacy, quieted their consciences with the fine things they had said, and proceeded to manufacture campaign material. It thus came about that David's just dealings were nothing more than extortion, and that his success was an affront to every neighbor who had not succeeded. Who was he, anyhow? Simply a poor country boy, who had got along in some mysterious way, and had now reached the eminence of a high place on the ticket, when there were older men in the district who should have had the honor. This talk pleased the older men, and although outwardly supporting David, they had hard feelings in their hearts, and listened to the talk against him with a complaisant air of secret gratification.

All this David saw and appreciated. He went to town, and had a long talk with Colonel Short. The colonel was affable and interested.

"I understand it perfectly," he said. "It is always that way, and we 'll have to whip those fellows into line. We 're going to have a pretty hard fight this year, and you must pile up a handsome majority in Sussex District to help us out. The best way is to begin by getting up the biggest meeting you have ever held. Your store at the Cross-roads is a central point, and there is no reason why you should not draw a crowd. Who is your worst man?"

"Old Silas Legg is about as bad as anybody. I traded horses with him once, and he never got over it."

"Yes; I know him. He is n't much account, but you can make him chairman of the meeting. How about the speakers?"

"There is Major Powderdry. We 'll have to have him, and yet if he gets started he 'll talk all night."

"And say nothing. Well, invent some means to shut him off. I 'll send Carr, and you can get some of your neighbors to make a few remarks, and your men to be in readiness to applaud. And above all things, get the more influential colored people there. We need some of their votes."

David went home, and began to make the arrangements. Notices were posted on trees and houses announcing.—

The Opening Gun of the Campaign.

Great Outpouring of the Citizens of Sussex.

All in Favor of Honest Government and Low Taxes Will Attend.

Eloquent Speeches by Major Hamilton Powderdry, Hon. Silas Legg, Hon. Erastus Crawley, Hon. Brent Carr.

Ladies Invited.

Freemen, Assert your Rights!

Save the County from Extravagance and Misrule!

Don't Forget the Place and Date.

Gad's Cross-roads, Thursday Night, Seven-Thirty O'Clock.

Come One, Come All!

A platform was constructed for the occasion. It was rough, but strong. In front were benches for the people.

Of course the meeting excited great interest. It offered a break in the dull routine of Sussex life, and the list of speakers gave a decided attraction to the programme. Moreover, mass-meetings in Sussex had some unexpected features that were worth seeing. Everything was fair in political warfare.

For days the orators advertised on the printed bills were full of varied emotions. Major Powderdry, more inflated than ever with his importance, rehearsed daily for his greatest effort. Silas Legg did n't think that he would go to the meeting at all, but his name in big letters on the posters was too much for his vanity. Erastus Crawley, after saying he would n't speak, drove his children out of his room because they interfered with some writing he was attending to, and that night he scared his wife nearly to death by jumping up in bed and shouting, "Fellow-citizens, I did not expect to make a speech, but —" He did n't get any further, for Mrs. Crawley pulled down his uplifted arm and asked him if he was crazy.

David contemplated his work Thursday morning with considerable satisfaction. Everything was ready. The weather was gloriously fair, the atmosphere was comfortable, and all the signs pointed to a great success. Sussex District did not boast a brass band, but the meeting itself would draw the people. The opposition were curiously quiet, and David was doubtful as to what tactics they would pursue. He had not forgotten the night, several years before, when they hid a hornets' nest under one of the benches, but he did not think they would try such a thing again; and even if they did, it was too late in the season for hornets to take much exercise. No; the matter which bothered him most was some way to cut off Major Powderdry's dull monotony of sound. He thought out various schemes, with no success at all, and then, taking recourse to his usual philosophy, he decided to wait for some kind fortune to help him out.

By seven o'clock the people had arrived. Along the road the carriages and wagons and horses made an imposing display. The benches were filled, crowds stood around the edges, and everybody was ready for the eloquence of the evening. Mrs. Ruth Gad, surrounded by the best ladies of the district, occupied seats well in front. Presently the distinguished speakers filled the chairs on the platform. David was there in his best suit of clothes. Silas Legg's linen was radiant and bountiful, and he held himself like a new school trustee at a female Commencement. Erastus Crawley had a conscious air, and occasionally his lips moved, as if he were trying to keep his impromptu speech well in memory. Young Carr sat with the easy grace of an experienced speaker, and, like a good politician, looked for his inspiration in the faces of the rosy-cheeked country girls in the audience. More prominent than all of these was Major Powderdry, who was trembling on the threshold of his greatest effort. He crossed and recrossed his legs until his trousers were in danger of being worn out. He talked first to one neighbor and then to another, and waited with great impatience until the party men of the district got seated on the stage. Then arising, and kicking down his trousers, which through too much movement had climbed above his shoe tops, he exhibited his large expanse of cuffs, and said, —

"Ladies and gentlemen, I move that the Honorable Silas Legg, our distinguished fellow-citizen, be made chairman of this splendid outpouring of the people."

The motion was seconded, and Mr. Legg, whose "honorable" had come from one brief term in the Legislature years before, arose, and slowly moved to the small table in front. He bowed to the applause, bowed to the platform, and bowed to the audience. Then, in a piping voice, he thanked the people for the compliment, and spoke of the pride of the district in the nomination of "that citizen whom we all love for his ability and integrity, Mr. David Gad, our next sheriff." There was great applause; and Ruth blushed, and felt very proud indeed that she had such a husband. Mr. Legg referred to the party; told the people that they ought to cast their votes "early but not often," and then said he would not delay the proceedings with any further remarks, but would introduce a man whom they all knew and all honored, — the Honorable Erastus Crawley.

Mr. Crawley, who likewise had been in the Legislature, moved to the front with easy grace. He raised his hand and began:

"Fellow-citizens, I did not expect to make a speech, but no man who loves his party as I love it can face this assemblage and wish to be quiet. It is a proud privilege to appear before you, and to say a few words in behalf of the splendid ticket that our party has placed in the field, — a ticket sound as a dollar and good as gold; a ticket which contains the name of our friend and neighbor David Gad, who will be our next sheriff when the setting sun shall fall upon the ides of November, and place upon our banners the insignia of victory."

The people did not take time to think how a setting sun was to put insignia on the banners; it was n't necessary; they simply saw Mr. Crawley's strong arm come down upon the table, and they heard his voice fall into a cadence that demanded applause, and they applauded. This roused the orator, and on he went, dealing out assurances of success and preaching party principles with rotund vehemence that called forth the liveliest manifestations of delight. Major Powderdry was getting still more fidgety, for he feared that Crawley would capture all the honors. Fortunately for his nerves, however, Mr. Crawley foundered. His memory gave out, and he had to jump over a whole section of his speech to the conclusion, which he delivered in the true war-horse style. He sat down, and with a big red handkerchief, which was reserved strictly for special occasions, wiped off the perspiration that had come from his sturdy oratory.

Both speeches had been brief. Then it was Major Powderdry's turn. Slowly and pompously he came to the front. At each stage of the applause his importance swelled. He bowed with the generous grace of a true orator.

"Mr. Chairman, ladies and gentlemen, fellow-countrymen, and fellow-citizens," he said, with noble impressiveness, as he raised his hand and again exhibited his immaculate cuff, "the assembled loveliness and yeomanry of proud old Sussex inspires me with the belief that the mighty voice of the sovereign people, speaking through the unerring medium of their patriotic enthusiasm, has ably and eloquently foreshadowed the splendid victory that will greet our magnificent old party in November." (Applause.)

This sentence would undoubtedly have ended more sonorously if Mr. Crawley had not snatched "the ides of November" from the major, and made him change his words. But fortunately the rest of the speech differed entirely from Mr. Crawley's, and the major had no difficulty in rolling off his long and tedious phrases. Once fully started, he was like a boat launched in the tide; he kept on going until — until —

Yes, until something happened. It was while he was growing eloquent over the "matchless and deathless principles of our glorious old party" that a strain of music with sundry shouts came from down the road, about a hundred yards away. The major drowned it with his voice; but up it came again, louder than ever. Quickly some secret telegraph spread it around that there was a performing bear in the vicinity. The news had a wonderful effect. At first, those on the outside slipped away. Then the benches began to be emptied. The major talked on with brave resolution; but what was a mere orator in a country district to a performing bear?

David Gad was in dismay. Only the women and a few men were left in the audience. His meeting was on the verge of failure. He called a man, and found out the trouble. He did not hesitate.

"Keep it going, gentlemen, till I get back," he said. And jumping off the platform, he hurried to the road.

The plotters of the opposition quickly mingled with the crowd when they saw him approaching. He came on, with his face full of determination. It had been many years since he had seen a bear, but his curiosity was overwhelmed in his desire to save the meeting.

There, in the centre of the crowd, the

poor old bear was dancing to the discord of an asthmatic bagpipe. David marched boldly into the arena and demanded the cause of the interference. The man promptly replied that he was on his way to town, and that some young gentlemen had paid him a dollar to give a performance.

"Come with me," whispered David, "and I'll give you two dollars; and if you don't come, I'll have you arrested."

The two dollars was a stronger inducement than the threat. Very promptly the man, leading the bear, followed David Gad, and behind them came the crowd that had forsaken the meeting.

The animal produced a great sensation. Major Powderdry took a recess; and when it was seen that David was going to have that bear give a brief performance on the platform, the excitement reached an intensity which had never been known in that neighborhood.

"He is harmless, gentlemen," was David's assurance; but it did not assure the distinguished committee-men and officers. They did not care to share the honors of the platform with a bear. Hon. Silas Legg surrendered the chairmanship, and became a humble spectator; Hon. Erastus Crawley thought he would rather see the proceedings from the audience; and Major Powderdry, with a look of supreme contempt, retired to the corner of the stage, where he could easily jump off at the first sign of hostility. David Gad remained bravely at his post.

"Ladies and gentlemen," he said, "we not only defy the opposition, but we capture their ammunition; and we are going to show you the kind of arguments that they use, by letting their animals give a little show." (Applause.)

David motioned to the man, and he came forward with the bagpipe and the bear. He played a tune — or an apology for a tune — and Bruin danced to the music. Everybody was attentive. The performance met with great applause, and a second instalment was called for. David had secured the undivided respect of every man and woman in the place.

"Now, ladies and gentlemen, we will have some more speech-making. Nothing like variety, you know."

The man and the bear retired. The animal lay down on the far corner of the platform. Major Powderdry saw the field open, and advanced to finish his speech. David was sorely disappointed. He had hoped the major would not try again; but the major was not the kind of man to spend a week over his greatest effort, and have it ruined by such untoward circumstances. He began at the safe corner of the platform, but his eloquence being of the moving sort — especially in its effects on himself — he gradually warmed up to his words and approached the centre of the stage. His oratory was never better. The audience was interested, and the bear was quiet. Presently he reached a climax that called for applause. It came vociferously. David joined in it by stamping on the platform. The bear woke up and growled. The major looked around, and seeing Bruin, promptly returned to his corner.

Again he proceeded. Again he waxed eloquent. Again there was applause. Again Bruin growled, and again the major retired from the centre of the stage to his corner.

A third time he started out to awake the echoes.

"In the multiplied industries, the diverse interests of our glorious nation," he said, "what party has afforded the most sacred security to our advancing progress? What principles, founded on justice and built by experience, compassing the munificent wisdom of past history with the magnificent practicalities of the golden age of the present, have given the rich incentives to our expanding civilization, the splendid promise of freedom and safety to our sovereign citizenship, and the sure protection against extravagance in our public affairs? What principles, I say,—and I repeat it with all the earnestness of my soul,—what principles, except those which are embodied, like jewels in rich settings of gold, in the platform and practices of our great and glorious old party?"

There was tremendous applause. The people clapped their hands and hurrahed. David stamped on the platform with all the force of his heavy new boots. And suddenly the bear, with a noisier growl than ever, arose to his feet, and made a step forward. The major heard him, and saw him advance. In his heated imagination, red hot from the fires of eloquence, he fancied a whole drove of bears coming upon him with distended jaws. He did not tarry, but with a leap cleared the stage, and took refuge in the audience.

Great excitement began, but a panic was easily averted by the man, who took hold of the chain and pulled the animal back.

David again came to the front. "That was a beautiful speech of Major Powderdry's," he said. "It was sound and reasonable and eloquent. Now, to show you a contrast, we'll have another of the sort of speeches our enemies use."

This reassured the people, who caught the full spirit of the fun. The music began, and the bear advanced in the usual way. While the performance was in progress David retired, and called some of his men to him.

"Get this man and this bear away from here," he whispered. "Drive them down the road, and threaten to hang the man to a tree if he don't get out of the neighborhood. And mind, do it quietly."

When the dance was over David took the man to the rear of the stage, and placed two dollars in his hand. As he did so he whispered, —

"Get away from here. Leave the neighborhood. If you don't, we'll string you to a tree."

The event had filled the poor wanderer with astonishment. He had been so dazed that he scarcely remembered his old tunes. The amazement kept on increasing, and this last admonition settled him. Grabbing the money and holding it tightly, he got off the platform, and pulled the bear after him. Then, plunging into the darkness, he fled from the place.

Quite promptly and complacently David came to the front again. He had bloomed out on the platform all at once. It surprised no one more than himself to find that he was talking in a good voice to so many people whom he had never faced collectively before. The excitement and the needs of the hour developed him. He introduced Mr. Carr with a vigorous flourish of compliments, and the young orator proceeded to give the people a strong, practical, persuasive speech, illustrated and brightened by good stories that kept every one amused and interested, his remarks being so entertaining that the bear was for the time forgotten.

It was getting rather late — late for the country, of course — when Carr finished; but he saw that the people were not especially tired, and he took David's breath away by saying that he was sure everybody wanted to hear a few words from the candidate for sheriff. He was shrewd enough to observe that David had in him a strong vein of eloquent common-sense. His handling of the bear incident showed that. David hesitated, but when the demand became urgent, he arose and tried to say something, looking to Ruth for his inspiration.

"Ladies and gentlemen," he began, "I am no speech-maker: but as the representative of this district on the ticket, I feel proud of the honor, and I tell you squarely that I want your votes. ("You 'll get 'em," shouted a voice.) I believe I will, my friend; and I tell you now that some people will have about as much success in downing our ticket as they did in trying to stop this meeting. (Great applause.) We 'll not only capture them, but their bears and all the other animals in their menagerie. (Renewed demonstrations.) Fellow-citizens, I 'd like to say one word about that bear. You noticed him did n't you? Did you ever see such a bear? (Laughter.) He was strong and healthy, and yet he looked poor and weak and ashamed — looked as if he had lost his self-respect and independence. Now think a minute. What does that bear do? He does all the work. He does the dancing, while the man with the wind-bag plays the music. So far so good. Now when the money comes in, who gets it, — the bear that makes the show a success, or the man with the wind? Why, the poor old bear don't get anything. If sugar-cured hams were a cent apiece, he would never know the taste of them in a year. (Laughter.) The man just plays, and the old bear dances, and I would n't wonder if he was fool enough to think that he was doing the right thing. (Laughter.) Now, it strikes me, fellow-citizens, that our friends on the other side have sent us a first-class specimen of their way of running their party. ("That's so!" said a voice.) I see before me some good members of that party, and I see some colored voters who belong to it, too. Now I ask them if their bosses have not been playing on the wind-bag, and making them do the dancing. (Laughter.) Have n't they cast the votes, while the bosses stood around and waited for the prizes? Who got the proceeds? Why, fellow-citizens of the other side of the fence, you have been doing all the work, and you have n't got a smell of the results. (Laughter and applause.) You are the bear, and the bosses are the firm that plays a little campaign music, and takes all the offices. (Great laughter.) Why don't you come into a party that treats you like men, that respects your independence and glories in your manhood? (Great applause.) You have heard the splendid speeches here to-night. These men talked to your reason; they did n't play on wind, and expect you to do the dancing while they put the money in their pockets, and left you to prowl around the corn-fields for your supper. (More laughter and renewed applause.) Come into an honest party. We 've already got a big majority, but there 's always room for more; and we will see that you will be treated like free American citizens, and not like animals to be trotted out once a year to do the voting for somebody else's profit. I thank you, ladies and gentlemen, for your kind attention."

There was n't any applause too fervent for David Gad. He had spoken in a homely, forcible way, carrying everybody with him. Mr. Legg's piping words, Mr. Crawley's tumultuous blows, Major Powderdry's voluble rhetoric, and even Carr's able arguments, were forgotten in the apt and telling illustration of the candidate for sheriff. The people were astonished at his performance, and were proud of his success, and they crowded to the front to shake him by the hand.

"David," said Carr, "that is worth a hundred votes."

But David shook his head, and began to

compliment the other speakers. He thanked the Hon. Silas Legg for his kindness and his eloquent words; he thanked the Hon. Erastus Crawley for his magnificent speech; he thanked Major Powderdry for his splendid address — "the best I ever heard, major; as fine as anything any orator could do."

And so everybody went home pleased and satisfied.

Carr spent the night at David Gad's. When all the people had gone, Carr and David and Ruth sat down to a little supper which Ruth had prepared. Ruth was prouder than ever of her husband.

"That bear was very funny," she said; "but it was too bad for it to scare poor Major Powderdry so! Was n't it, Mr. Carr?"

Carr looked at David, and noticed a vagrant smile steal over his face.

"David, how did you manage it?" he asked.

"Oh, I did n't do anything! There was a loose board on the platform. I was sitting on one end of it and the bear was on the other end, and somehow when I applauded, the board flew up and hit the bear, and the bear did n't seem to like it. Carr," exclaimed

David, "that bear saved the meeting. Some kind Providence sent him here to-night. If it had n't been for him, the major would have talked all night."

Ruth laid down her knife and fork, and gazed sadly at her husband.

"David," she said, as she shook her head, "I 'm afraid politics will be the ruination of you."

But Carr declared that it was the best thing he had ever heard of, and he accused David of having the bear around on purpose; but David denied this, and said it was nothing but pure good-luck, "which," he added, "is better than riches, and is just as good as a campaign fund."

THE ELECTION.

MATTERS did not go as well with the candidacy of David Gad as the beginning had promised. Even the great mass-meeting did not reassure the success which was so certain at first.

With his good wife Ruth he was sitting in the parlor. He seemed disconsolate. Ruth busied herself with sewing, while he gazed alternately at the lamp and floor.

" David," said Ruth, " something is troubling you."

" Yes, dear; something usually is."

" You have n't any doubt about your election, have you ? "

" Of course not. Did you ever know a candidate to have any doubts except as to the size of his majority ? "

" Now I know something 's wrong. What is it ? "

David did not answer. He looked steadily and sturdily at the floor. Ruth waited awhile, and then resumed: —

"What is it, David? You have n't been comfortable since the mail came in yesterday."

David glanced up quickly. "Ruth," he said, "did you ever see through a brick wall?"

"The idea of such a question! I believe you are losing your mind. You 've lost about everything else since you got into politics."

"Yes," responded the candidate for sheriff, gloomily; "and I 'm going to lose more."

Ruth dropped her sewing and gazed at him in open-eyed dismay. "What!" she asked, "do they want money? Why, they declared it should n't cost you anything."

David shook his head sadly. "It 's always that way," he said. "They sugar-coat you with compliments, and for every compliment they issue a note that you 've got to pay before the campaign ends. This politics, Ruth, is a great scheme to use a man's vanity for opening his pocket-book. It 's got so that I 'm afraid to hear a man praise me, lest he should come around afterward to borrow money, and I 'm disappointed if he does n't come, because I feel sure he 's going to vote against me."

"Now, David, if they said that you would strengthen the ticket, and if that is why they put you on, why don't they go ahead and elect you?"

"Bless your innocent soul, Ruth, you don't know politics! Six weeks ago they all said I'd go through with flying colors, and everybody was crowding around promising to put up money and help me, but six weeks in politics is about six years longer than eternity."

"Did n't they contribute as they said they would?"

"Yes, some did, — Major Powderdry for one."

"Major Powderdry! Why, David, I never knew that he contributed to anything except his debts."

"That's about what he did. It was this way. Three weeks ago the major came around and said he wanted to make a good contribution to the campaign fund, and after a lot of a-hemming and a-hawing he asked me to lend him a hundred dollars on his note. As long as I had taken the nomination from him, and as the money would help my own election, I loaned it to him."

"And he contributed it to the fund?"

David smiled grimly. "Yes, twenty-five

of it. He put the other seventy-five in his pocket. It was the first time that I ever knew Major Powderdry was a financier."

"A financier!" exclaimed Ruth, indignantly; "I call it robbery."

"No, my dear; it 's finance. As far as I can see, finance is the general barter of humanity, and the biggest financier is the fellow who manages to hold on to the most money. Now old Canton is another financier. We made him chairman of our first mass-meeting, and gave him enough honor for his whole family. Of course we expected to get a good contribution from him. Well, he promised and promised. Then he kept saying that times was hard, and it all ended by his handing over five dollars out of his fifty thousand. And now he is lending me money, and making me pay twelve per cent interest on it. The old skinflint will make nearly a hundred dollars out of me."

Ruth did not know much about politics, but she had helped David in the store enough to understand something about the rules of interest. This disclosure evidently alarmed her.

"Do you mean to say," she asked, "that you have put a thousand dollars into this thing?"

"As the day of execution is near at hand, my dear, I suppose I'd just as well confess. A thousand is about the size of it."

"But, David, I don't see where you can use all the money."

"Campaign expenses," he answered, sententiously.

"What are they?"

"Printing tickets and mass-meetings and hiring music, and — and other things."

"What other things? You don't mean to say, David, that you pay to get votes?"

"Certainly not, my dear; but some people have to be persuaded."

"Persuaded?"

"Yes, persuaded. There are lots of men who will vote our ticket, but they must be paid for their loss of time. Now, for instance, there is Bill Simpson. Bill will vote for our ticket, but he needs persuasion. He wants five dollars for his loss of time in going to the polls."

"But, David, you know that he never does anything, and how can his time be valuable?"

"That's just it. His time isn't valuable except when elections come round. Then everybody finds out that it is a very busy season, and that it will be hard to get to the voting places unless the party does something for him. I went to see Bill. He said he certainly wanted to vote for me, but he did not see how he was going to get away, for he had a big job of work to do, and it would be worth every cent of five dollars for him to lay off and go to the polls. What are you going to do with such a man unless you compromise?"

"Compromise?"

"Yes, compromise. "He 'll really expect about two dollars. Last year he got one."

"David," said Ruth, after a pause, "is n't it wrong to do this?"

"It may not be exactly right, dear, but it 's painfully necessary. At election time every man is as big as every other man, and his vote counts just the same whether he is a President or a loafer."

Ruth paused again while her thoughts struggled for utterance. Presently she said:

"David, I 'd rather see you defeated than do anything that is not right. I hope and pray that you do not think of buying votes."

"Of course not, of course not," he replied, with some warmth. "What put such an idea into your head? And, moreover, what would be the use of trying? The other fellows have the most money."

"How do you know?"

"That's what the letter said, and that's what has been troubling me. Why, Ruth, the unprincipled scoundrels have three hundred new two-dollar notes for use on Tuesday. Just think of it! That's enough to carry this district against the Angel Gabriel! And if I lose Sussex, I lose the election and my thousand dollars. It's awful."

Ruth quickly jumped from criticism to sympathy. She wanted David to be elected, and she had thought he would be until now, when the prospect seemed to change.

"If women only had the right to vote!" was all she could say at first.

David smiled sardonically. "Yes," he said,—"if they could. It's always 'if.' If wishes were two-dollar notes I'd be satisfied."

In his perturbation he picked up the paper that was lying on the table and began to read, while Ruth returned to her sewing. There was silence for some minutes until David called for the scissors. Ruth handed them to him, and he cut a paragraph from the sheet.

"Ruth, how many people around here take the 'Sussex Weekly'?"

She named several.

"Well, to-morrow morning I want you to go to all the houses and get the papers. I need them."

"What is it, David?"

"Oh, nothing much. You know I always make it a rule to cut things out that strike my fancy, and I find in the long run that a newspaper is the best investment that I make, because it gives me more new ideas than anything else. I calculate that this little piece of paper is worth a hundred dollars, if not more."

He folded it carefully and placed it in his pocket-book.

The next morning after breakfast Ruth started out to visit her neighbors to borrow the "Sussex Weekly." She succeeded in bringing back five copies. David was delighted. At dinner she questioned him again, but his only reply was, —

"Come down in the store when I close to-night and you will see."

It was a busy day. The next morning the election was to begin. Visitors came constantly to consult the candidate for sheriff. Tricks and rumors of tricks were in the air. Workers wanted money. All asked favors. Everybody whispered fears of defeat in the private office, and boasted of victory to the crowd in front of the store. Major Powderdry, radiant in his optimism, and exhaustless in his declarations of success, was there.

"We will sweep the county as clean as the celestial dome," he said, "and proud old Sussex will lead the districts in the great battle of free government and low taxes. Gentlemen," — nodding to several smiling members of the opposition, — "you 'd better join the army, and march through the sea of politics with the children of Israel, for, sure as you 're born, it's going to be a damp season for the Egyptians. Take the advice of a friend, and get in out of the wet by voting for David Gad."

"Major," replied one of the opposition, "there was an Irishman once who happened in a field where there was a large, healthy bull. He pulled out a red handkerchief, and the bull began kicking and bellowing. It was very funny. The Irishman laughed so loud that he had to hold his sides. But suddenly the bull came close, and when Paddy picked himself up on the other side of the fence he said, sadly, 'It's a mighty good thing I got that laugh in first.'"

"My dear fellow," said the major, impressively, "I have profound respect for the age of your story, but excuse me if I say that it does n't fit the case. To-morrow we shall take that bull by the horns and lead him to the slaughter like a frightened lamb that has been fed on mint sauce just to whet our appetites."

The major was in his element, and he kept up his fire of repartee with undiminished vigor. Everybody talked about the morrow. Presently somebody discovered a newspaper clipping pasted on a board placed rather inconspicuously near the desk of the store.

"Hello, David, what 's this?"

"What 's what?"

"This newspaper article?"

"Oh, that! I suppose it is something that John has stuck up for reference."

Of course the people crowded around to see what it was. This is what they read:

"LOOK OUT FOR BAD MONEY!

"We are informed that a lot of counterfeit two-dollar notes are in circulation in this State, and some of them have found their way into this county. The bank officers tell us that they are so clearly and perfectly engraved that it is difficult for anybody who is not an expert to tell the differences from the real article. Of course our readers know that it is a crime punishable by imprisonment to attempt to pass these notes, and there is a reward for the arrest of everybody caught in the act. We advise you all to be careful about this thing. Beware of new two-dollar notes."

They read it carefully, and wanted to know its meaning. David was very ignorant about it.

"John 's simply stuck it up there, I guess. John 's a little absent-minded sometimes, and he wants something to keep him from taking in another counterfeit. He took in one, and he looks as if he 'd been to a funeral ever since."

"You don't think that any of the bills are around here?" put in one of David's political opponents, rather experimentally.

"No; not that I know of. All the two-dollar notes I 've seen this week are old, and of course they 're all right."

The hour of breaking up came, and the people started for their homes. As they left the store, Major Powderdry stood on the highest step and indulged in more rhetoric.

"To-morrow's setting sun," he said, "is going to witness a sight that will cast new glory on the American eagle. Victory will perch on our standards, and our ticket will go through like a streak of greased lightning. Sleep well, gentlemen, and be at the polls early."

"We 'll be there," shouted the major's opponents.

After they had gone and the shutters were put up, Ruth came downstairs. She looked around until she discovered the clipping pasted on the board.

"Is that it?" she asked.

"Yes," said David, "that 's it."

Good weather blessed the day of election. The people were up early. Around the polls was plenty of life and noise. An election in a rural district differs entirely from an election in the city. Your city people walk to the polls, cast their ballots, and walk away. The highest privilege of citizenship is a matter for expedition. In the country it is an occasion for assembling, for gossip and argument and entreaty. Along the road are carriages and horses, ox-carts, wagons, and all the curious kinds of vehicles of the neighborhood. The voters stop to talk and to consult. No hurry disturbs them. They stand around, some whip in hand, some holding tickets, some smoking bad cigars, and all personally interested in the contest. The fences are the reserved seats of the occasion. Up the road in quiet corners are the practical workers, with the sinews of war. Behind trees are jugs and bottles of dangerous inspiration. A mercenary voter is never in haste to vote. He canvasses the situation, finds out the resources of both sides, gets frequent exhilaration from the jugs and the bottles, and finally casts his ballot with the largest pecuniary benefit to himself. The efforts of the workers to monopolize this individual are earnest, prolonged, and untiring.

It was this way in Sussex District. David Gad's friends made a cordon around the polls. The candidate for sheriff was not present at his polling-place, except for a short time to cast his vote, but he was ably represented. The opponents, however, were just as strong, and were all the more dangerous because they remained in the quiet corners up the road where they could barter without discovery.

In David's store matters were quiet, as the chief interest centred at the polls. John was ostensibly in charge. David kept watchfully and quietly in the background. He was waiting for developments. About half-past eight o'clock he saw a figure coming from the voting-place, and his heart beat more excitedly with anticipation. The man was a surly fellow named Higgs, an unconscionable bribe-taker.

Higgs entered the store, which was the only one near the polls, and bought some tobacco. In payment he proffered a new two-dollar note.

"No you don't," said John.

"Don't what?"

"We ain't taking no bad money here."

"What do you mean?" said the fellow, with a mixture of indignation and alarm.

"This is what I mean," said John, and taking down the board, he read the article about counterfeits.

Higgs was dumfounded. Then he recovered his powers of speech, and deluged the place with his surcharged feelings. In the midst of it David appeared.

"Good-morning, Mr. Higgs. It 's a pleasant day for the election. Have you voted?"

Without replying, Higgs called himself various unprintable names, and told David how he had been imposed upon by some unnamed scoundrel.

"This is very serious," said David. "Of course you thought the money was good, and I don't believe you would want to run the danger of getting arrested by trying to pass a counterfeit. But if I were you I 'd make the fellow who gave it to you pay for it with interest."

Higgs, with unmistakable emphasis, declared he would, and left the store in hot haste. He had just disappeared around the bend of the road when Major Powderdry drove up and dismounted. He rushed to the store, and led David into the back shed.

"It 's all right," he said. "Our men have got the articles at every polling-place, and they 're going to raise the devil just as soon as a two-dollar note appears. How are things here?"

"Higgs has just been in with a two-dollar note, which we refused to accept."

"Good!"

"And he 's gone back to the polls to see about it. He 's hotter than a tin roof in August."

"That 's simply magnificent. I 'm going down there to help him. You stay here."

The major was lost in a cloud of dust. He urged his horse on until he came near the voting-place, and then slowed up and approached with an easy dignity which seemed to indicate that he had only a passing interest in the momentous events of the day.

But he did not remain passive. All around him the people were talking excitedly. Higgs's voice was loud in anger. His charges were taken up by the other rascals who, like himself, had sold their suffrages for two dollars each. The managers of the opposition tried entreaty and pacification, and it looked as if they were making some headway until Major Powderdry jumped into the breach. His face flushed, his fists beat the air, his voice rang out in fury. The people crowded around him.

"It is the most atrocious outrage I ever heard of," he exclaimed. "These men try to pollute the fame and corrupt the citizenship of this district; they insult every honest voter here; and not only that, but they impose on their victims by giving them worthless money. Gentlemen, I repeat that it is the most damnable affront that was ever offered to the decent sentiment of the sovereign people. Where is the man who will swear out warrants against these persons?"

In the face of the indignation the opponents beat a retreat to an obscure corner of the road where they could consult. Major

Powderdry took charge of the work. Every arrival was deluged with stories of the worthless money, was told how the opponents of David Gad were trying to defeat him by debauching and bribing voters, and was led to the polls through a line of David Gad's friends. The other side did not recover from the set-back; it could not cope with the tireless energy and exhaustless adjectives of Major Powderdry.

And so the work went bravely on until — until —

Major Powderdry, dust-covered and husky, rushed into the house of David Gad. It was past sunset, and the voting was over. David jumped forward to hear the result.

"Not yet — not yet," exclaimed the major, with a majestic wave of his oratorical arm. "Bring out your demijohn — your large demijohn. I have four acres of dust and five summer fogs in my throat, and I 'm doomed to certain death unless I get a drink within the next five minutes."

David supplied the demand with welcome alacrity.

"Consider yourself decorated with a life-saving medal," said the major.

"Now tell me how it all went."

"You know when I left here this morning?"

"Yes."

"Well, as soon as I arrived there I began to raise thunder, and, by Jove, we kept it raised until the polls closed! We simply knocked the other side out on the first round. The fates favored us when Higgs came up to the store. When he got back, he bellowed like a bull, and the more he bellowed the more we egged him on, and pretty soon we had things our own way. I discovered that about five or ten years ago Cartridge, who was handling the money for the other side, had got mixed up in some of that green-goods business in one of the cities; he was innocent undoubtedly, but that did n't make any difference. I went up to him and whispered: 'Look here, Mr. Cartridge, you can't come any of your green-goods game on these people. We want a fair election, and we 're going to have it. If you pay out any more of those two-dollar notes we 'll put you in the penitentiary, and keep you there till your head gets bald!'"

"What did he say?"

"Nothing. I did n't give him time to say anything. We were too busy keeping up the cry of bribery and counterfeit to discuss side issues. We laid it on heavy. The people backed me up nobly. I talked more than I ever did in all my life. As the voters came up, we never let them go until we gave them the whole story with a lot of ornament. We told them of the plot to defeat you, and let them know plainly that the decent people were not going to allow any such an outrage. And the negroes! Oh, David, you ought to have seen how we managed them! I got hold of Big Jim, for I knew he had more influence with his race than any one else, and promised him that you would pay him five dollars to-morrow if he would scare the negroes with the counterfeit story, and keep them away from those new two-dollar notes. It worked beautifully. The other fellows are swearing like pirates. They 're beaten. I know that we have carried this district."

"But how about the county?"

"I haven't heard a word. Let 's wait awhile, and see if we can get any news."

They waited. In an hour the result of that precinct came in. The counting of the vote had been completed. It gave David a majority of one hundred and sixty-seven, — fully one hundred more than he expected. An hour later a rider brought news from the adjoining voting-place. The counterfeit dodge had worked successfully. David had a majority there of forty-five, when he did not expect more than fifteen or twenty. Matters looked bright. About ten o'clock a messenger from the opposite direction arrived. He came from the district adjoining the county town. The counterfeit dodge had been a failure. As soon as it was sprung, the workers had rushed on horseback into town, and had their new money changed for old. They got back without much loss of time, and swept the district against David by a majority of two hundred and eighty-four.

"I 'm nearly dead," exclaimed the major, "but I can't stand this. I 'm going to town."

Others joined him, and off they started at full gallop. David remained at home. If he was elected, all well and good; if not, he was n't going to be in town to let the people see his disappointment.

He and Ruth went to bed, but not to sleep. He tried to feel calm, but his mind refused to be quiet. He turned and twisted. His eyes would not stay closed. The clock struck the hours. Time seemed to crawl along. Four o'clock came. Toward five the minutes were travelling when he heard the sound of horses' hoofs coming at breakneck speed up the road. A minute more there was a halt before his store, and a mighty shout of "Hurrah for Gad!"

Above the din was the major's voice, "Come out, David."

David appeared at the window in short order, and as soon as his white-robed form was seen, the shouts were trebled in vigor. The major tried to make a speech, and his companions tried to help him, but it was not a brilliant success. They were full of very bad liquor, and David was full of the emotions of a man who has run his first campaign and won.

"Come away from that window, or you 'll catch cold," said a small, shrill voice; but David did not hear.

He stood there listening to the revelry. By and by the revellers got tired, and with more hurrahs started on their way, making the night hideous as they went with bacchanalian sounds, which might be interpreted into something about not going home until morning.

David felt proud of the exhibition, but Ruth lost no time in declaring that it was scandalous.

A week later David and Ruth were sitting in their room. The store had been closed for the night. In the fireplace the logs burned lazily, and the shaded lamp sent its rays upon Ruth's knitting and David's newspaper.

"I am certainly thankful it's all over," said Ruth. "I had n't any peace from the time the campaign started. But I'm truly glad that you are elected, and it did my heart good to read the fine things that the newspaper said about you. And yet, David, I feel rather sorry in having to leave this store and our old friends."

"We won't leave them all, dear. I saw Major Powderdry to-day, and told him that I would like to do something to show my appreciation of his work, but the best I could do was to offer him the position of deputy, which I would be very glad if he would accept."

"Did he?"

"Yes; he accepted. He's been after an office for twenty years, and this is the first real chance that he has had, so he did not let it escape. And speaking of the major reminds me that we took in three of those new two-dollar notes to-day. I gave one to John. Here is one that I want you to frame with that newspaper clipping, as a souvenir of our first campaign."

"And the other?"

"I guess I'll send that to renew my subscription to the 'Sussex Weekly.'"

A NEW DEAL.

"WHAT'S this? 'Hand-Book of Etiquette!' Well, well!" and he opened the volume. "Forms of declination!" he read again. "'Mr. and Mrs. De Dash regret extremely that they are unable to accept the polite invitation of Mr. and Mrs. De Blank.' It's too bad! I wonder if they've got measles in the family, or perhaps the children are down with the croup. Now look here, my dear, if you're going to get fashionable, I'll resign, and go back to Gad's Crossroads."

David Gad was not the first man who found something amusing in a book on etiquette, and as long as a sense of humor remains with the human race, he will not be the last. But in the case of himself and his wife Ruth there was a special significance. They were on the threshold of a new career. He had been elected sheriff of Quantico County. He had established

Major Powderdry, his deputy, in the jail residence, and for himself and Ruth had taken a house in a desirable section of Salem, the county-seat.

Salem was a place of two thousand people, mostly politicians; but while it was small, it was exacting in its social demands. Family was greater than wealth, although wealth was occasionally accepted as a substitute for ancestry. With the Gads the situation was in the middle; their antecedents were humble but reputable, and their means were the comfortable results of attention to business and economy. In Sussex District they were as good as other people, but in the county town they had the disadvantage of newness. David's election had made him known, and he was geographically immortalized in the naming of Gad's Crossroads, but he knew that the best success under the changed circumstances must come from a policy of prudence. He idolized Ruth, he believed her better than the best, and he had the fullest confidence in her social possibilities. So while he made fun of the "Hand Book of Etiquette," he was secretly elated by its presence in the house.

Their town life began as an experiment, and grew on observation. Everything was new. It was the step from the informality of rural intercourse, in which everybody knew everybody, to the clearly defined circles of an organized society. Salem had an aristocracy. The aristocrats were proud of their transatlantic ancestries, proud of the official honors that had come to their names in the republic. In their life they mingled the consciousness of their origin with a superiority of the present that demanded a dignified standard of conduct and a general recognition of their family importance.

In Salem, politics followed the lines of society as closely as possible. Many of the aristocrats depended upon office for their incomes. The intelligence of the county concentrated in the town manipulated affairs so as to secure the choicest results for its favorites. Sometimes there were signs of revolt in the outlying districts, and occasionally rural leaders became so strong that danger was threatened, but the bosses at Salem — "the court-house crowd" — were full of policy and pacification.

Colonel Short, who was the chief of the bosses, was a man of middle age, close in his dealings, but zealously alert in his personal habits. In many respects he was an ideal politician of the practical sort. He was well posted. He studied men, managed them by their vanities, and saved himself in emergencies by adroitly allowing candidates to fight one another instead of assailing him. David Gad's name was placed on the ticket in this peculiar manner. There was a scramble for the sheriff's office. None of the scramblers suited Colonel Short. David had commended himself by his reticence, his good sense, and his service as a secret handler of campaign funds. Colonel Short and he talked it over. The sheriff's office was promised to him. The agreement was a mutual confidence. Not a word was said, but in a few weeks nearly every district in the county had a candidate, and when the convention met they fought each other beyond the hope of peace. It was then that Colonel Short, in his capacity of peacemaker, got Major Powderdry to withdraw as the candidate of Sussex District, and substitute the name of Gad, who was there as one of the major's delegates. The startled look of feigned astonishment that David showed to the cheering convention was to Colonel Short one of the most delightful experiences in all his political career, and the fact that David, now installed as sheriff, had Major Powderdry as the chief deputy added to his appreciation of the episode.

Next to Colonel Short in power was Mr. Presford, who for sixteen consecutive years had enjoyed the fees of the clerkship of the Circuit Court. He was the politest man in the county, a dispenser of cordiality that occasionally cheered but never compromised. An illustrious ancestry, comprising an officer in the Revolutionary army, a foreign minister, and a member of Congress, illumined his social importance. His wife, with family connections equalling his own, was the leader of the county society, and her house was the centre of its aristocracy. To Mr. Presford there was a place for politics and a place for society, and he objected to desecrating his home for electioneering purposes. He looked upon David Gad as one of the incidents of politics. Secretly it may have pained him to see the party conferring its offices on persons of inferior pedigree, but he was too polite and too politic to confess to the feeling, and, moreover, the party had to do something occasionally for the common people or it might lose their votes.

Around Colonel Short and Mr. Presford were a dozen lawyers of varying ages, some of whom held offices, and all of whom were looking for larger opportunities. Henry Carr was the most prominent. He was a fine fellow, with a plenty of natural eloquence, a sturdy manhood, and an unusual equipment of that rare but valuable quality in politics —patience. The aristocrats confidently expected to hear his voice in Congress. A contrast to Carr was little Dickey Binson, a small but active aristocrat, who dressed better and put on more style with his few hundred dollars salary as a copying clerk under his uncle, Mr. Presford, than the richest man in the county. Dickey's chief ambition in life was to talk family, dance all night, and draw his salary in advance. Carr appreciated David Gad's qualities. Dickey thought it a base presumption for an "old hayseed" to try to enter the town's society.

David Gad was blissfully unconscious of the emotions that his coming had aroused. He had always made it a rule to attend to his own business, and he and Ruth thought mainly of getting settled in their home. Ruth's natural good taste was quick to appreciate and utilize suggestions, and the result was that within a month their house was in excellent order.

By that time, too, the neighbors had begun to visit them. Among the first were Senator and Mrs. Boone, who lived on the opposite side of the street, and who belonged to the best society of the town. It was foreordained that Ruth and Mrs. Boone, both of whom were great home-bodies, should at some time in their lives come together. At first they seemed a little scared at each other, but the moment they began to talk flowers and preserves, they felt very comfortably acquainted. When they got so as to exchange recipes and patterns and cook-books, they reached that domestic affinity that smoothed all thoughts into a perfect harmony of feeling; and when Mrs. Boone was sick for three days, and Ruth prepared jellies for her and spent the afternoon at her bedside, the friendship grew into that strong if somewhat occasional reciprocity that makes one family refer to another as "the best of neighbors."

Men have no such short-cuts to intimacy. They cannot exchange patterns and recipes and make jellies for one another. But in some way David and the senator got along wonderfully well. They spent many evenings together. The senator was a lawyer of long experience with men and affairs, —

a citizen whose sharp interest in public matters was more in the abstract than in personal participation, although he had been a member of the State Senate, the title of which honor still clung to his name.

"I was very sorry that you refused a second term," said David one evening. "You were the truest representative that the county has had since I can remember. If your plans had been carried out, we would have the old-time majority and the old-time enthusiasm."

"I am glad to hear you say that, Mr. Gad. You appreciate as well as I do how methods have changed. We have bossism here in its worst form. Our politics have become a scramble for office, and our friends in town are manipulating them so that they always get the rewards. Money has taken the place of merit, and promises made only to be broken are more powerful than principles. I was placed on the ticket to save it, but when success came to us, and I tried to introduce a few reforms in our county government, I found all the influences arrayed against me. I wanted to abolish the fee system in our offices, and substitute salaries; I wanted strict examination of accounts and a better election law — all of which the bosses opposed. They were stronger than I. And so our high taxes go on, our county is mismanaged, and the people's money finds its way into private pockets. By the way, I understand that you had quite an experience with those managers?"

"In what way?" asked David, utterly upset by the remark.

"Oh, because I know them so well," replied Senator Boone, with a smile. "See if I can guess the *modus operandi*. Last summer the outlook was bad. The opposition were active, and were loaded with first-class campaign ammunition. The court-house crowd became frightened. They needed a majority in Sussex District to carry them through. They looked around, and settled on Mr. David Gad. He was a man who stood well, who had done good, quiet service in politics, who had no antagonisms, and who possessed a few thousand dollars laid aside for a rainy day. Mr. Gad was invited to a conference with Colonel Short. The office was promised to him as a gift, without a cent of cost. He was nominated by a clever ruse that made the result appear entirely unpremeditated. It was after the nomination that Mr. Gad's troubles began. He had to work like a plough-horse, and he had to go down into his pockets; for after his nomination he would rather have spent all he possessed than be defeated." The senator paused a moment, and then resumed: "And I very strongly suspect that the nomination offered to Mr. Gad so free of expense made quite a little hole into a thousand dollars."

David's face was a study during the senator's diagnosis. All he could say was, "Senator, you will have to guess again."

"Not two thousand!" he exclaimed.

"No; just about twelve hundred and fifty."

And both men laughed.

"Mr. Gad, it is not the best of good taste to give a man advice without his asking for it, especially if the giver be a lawyer; but I hope you will keep your eyes well opened while you are in Salem."

In less than a week from the evening of this conversation, David received a note from Colonel Short asking him to come to his office. He was welcomed with marked cordiality. The usual greetings drifted into remarks upon current topics, until the colonel reached a personal point.

"It was one of the greatest pleasures of my life, Mr. Gad," he said, "to be instrumental in having you nominated and elected, and I am very glad to know that you are so comfortably settled in town. I should have been delighted to go on your bond, but you had it all arranged before I could offer my services."

David thanked him.

"Of course you know," he continued, "that I hold no office. I give my time and money to the party management because I want to see our party victorious and our county in safe hands. I ask no rewards for my work, but I have thought, Mr. Gad, that if you could do me a favor occasionally, we might work together in some matters."

David bowed his head, but said nothing.

"You remember," went on the colonel, in his blandest tones, "that when we agreed on the nomination last summer, we also agreed to stand by each other. My part of the contract, you know, has been faithfully carried out."

David remembered it. He also remembered the twelve hundred and fifty dollars. What he said, however, had no apparent relation to these thoughts.

"In what way, colonel, can I serve you?" he asked.

"Now we are coming to it. It is in your power as a sheriff to give to me as a lawyer a great many important cases, a service which will in no way compromise you, and which will enable you and me to work together. As long as I have no office, it is only fair that I should get these indirect favors from our party."

"Is that all?"

"Well, of course I may ask you once in a while to give special attention to some legal matters that may fall into your hands. They will give you little trouble, and will be in the strict line of your duty."

There was a pause, which was broken by David's rising to go.

"I believe we understand each other," said the colonel.

"Yes," said David, "I understand it;" and thanking the colonel for inviting him to call, he left the office.

The next evening David went over to see his neighbor. They were together in the library. The conversation was mainly on politics and county affairs.

"Senator," said David, "I have been looking into things down at the court-house in a quiet way, and I was wondering to-day what the control of all the county offices was worth. Now, take my place, — the sheriff's work and his influence?"

Senator Boone's eyes twinkled. "It is hard to say, but I suppose from six to ten thousand dollars would be a fair estimate for all the offices, and about three or four thousand for the sheriff's office, although in some years it is worth five, provided the sheriff devotes all patronage to one lawyer, and gives that enviable gentleman precedence in all legal matters. Do you want a partner?"

"Oh, no," laughed David. "If I should, I 'll advertise for bids."

"The only difficulty about it," said the Senator, "is that it is a big risk for the sheriff's reputation, and is rather against his oath of office; but of course a little thing like that does n't count in our modern politics."

David and Ruth soon had a comfortable circle of acquaintances, and their town life was altogether pleasant. The fact that the aristocrats, excepting Senator and Mrs. Boone, had not called disturbed them little. Indeed, they never mentioned it to each other.

After Lent the Presfords sent out invitations to a reception and dance. The coming event was the talk and the expectation of Salem society. Three days before it occurred, David started into the clerk's office on a matter of business. As he reached the door he stopped suddenly to see if he had his memorandum with him, and as he pulled his papers from his pocket he heard a voice say, —

"Dick, why did n't your uncle ask the Gads?"

"Oh, come now, dear boy, one has to draw the line somewhere, you know. Just because Gad was elected sheriff is no reason why he should be embraced socially. If you begin that sort of thing, what 's society going to amount to?"

David heard no more. He turned on his heel and walked away. That night at supper he acted more tenderly than usual toward Ruth.

"What have you to do to-morrow, dear?" he asked.

"Nothing in particular."

"Well, I 'm glad to hear it. You can go up to Sussex with me, can't you?"

"Yes, David, and I 'll be very glad to go."

"Then suppose we spend four days there. I 've got some business around the district, and it will take you and the other women that long to trade gossip."

When they returned — after a very pleasant visit — the Presford reception was over, and David resumed his work as if the greatest social event of the season had not ruffled the surface of the town.

With Powderdry, however, the case was different. He had not been invited, and he resented the slight. "My family is as good as Presford's," he declared; "and he need n't think he is so much better than the Powderdrys just because he has more money than I have."

David drew him aside. "Powderdry," he said, "don't make a fool of yourself. That kind of talk hurts you ten times as much as it hurts Presford."

But if Powderdry accepted David's advice in this respect, he did not stop his tongue in other matters. His work took him over the county. Country people always want to know what is going on in town, and Major Powderdry was quite willing to accommodate them.

"The court-house crowd are running things with a pretty high hand," he declared, "and are living like lords off the money of the tax-payers. Old Short and Presford have the best of it. If Senator Boone's plan of salaries, which he wanted to get through the Legislature, was in force they would not have half the money that they now have, and you people would have lower taxes. We fellows who have worked for the party all our lives hardly get enough to live on."

"How's David Gad?" they asked.

"Oh, he's all right, but he don't seem to suit the bosses. He runs his office honestly, and they don't like it. I tell you, gentlemen, if we had more of him in office the country would be better off. I know for a fact that he has saved a dozen of the people by giving them a little time and keeping off the mortgage-holding lawyers."

Reports of this talk soon found its way back to Salem. The bosses were quick to appreciate its influence. They had hitherto negatived criticism by having their own men talk it down, and ascribe it to the campaign lies of the opposition. They had long deceived the farmers and villagers. Powderdry's remarks were doubly dangerous. They must stop them.

Short and Presford sent for David. He came at the appointed time.

"Mr. Gad," said Colonel Short, "we have a complaint to make."

"Gentlemen, I'm all attention," replied the sheriff.

"Your deputy has been going around the county peddling a lot of nonsense that will hurt the party if his mouth is not closed."

"It will be pretty hard to do that," said David, with a smile.

"But it 's got to stop," said Presford.

"Yes," joined Short, "and it must stop right away. We gave you this office."

"*You* gave it to me, gentlemen?" asked David, with innocent emphasis.

"If it had not been for us you would never have gotten it. And since you have been there you have done nothing for us. You appointed Powderdry without consulting us. You run its affairs without asking our advice. You —"

There was a slight pause. David uncrossed his legs, and looking directly at Colonel Short asked, "What do you want?"

"You must discharge Powderdry."

"Yes, and you must discharge him at once," added Presford.

David arose. "Gentlemen," he said, with considerable firmness in his voice, "who is sheriff of this county?"

"Oh, there 's no use getting angry about it," said the colonel, quickly.

"Of course not, of course not. I 'm not at all angry, neither are you, but let me say that as long as I 'm sheriff, Powderdry remains my deputy."

There is a kind of atmospheric electricity pervading the politics of all county towns. The air in Salem was heavily charged with it, and gradually the office-holders became satisfied that the usual currents were not working regularly. Powderdry had felt that something was going on, and that in some mysterious way he was connected with it. So he asked David.

"Come around to my house after supper," replied the sheriff.

Powderdry came. The very fact of his punctuality was a strange exhibition of the ways of politics. Six months before, Powderdry, living proudly on his ancestry and his debts, looked upon David Gad as nothing more than a humble storekeeper. He expected to be the county sheriff, but David stepped in and got the office, and now he was serving as an underling of the man he once affected to patronize. He was much older than David; he had been in politics all his life; but he had talked more than he had schemed, and the result had been continuous defeat, until David had taken compassion on his twenty-five years of failure, and appointed him a deputy.

In politics talk is costly, silence is valuable. To know just how much to say, and how to say it, is beyond the price of rubies and fine jewels.

David was not in a hurry to open the conversation. This increased Powderdry's anxiety.

"What I tell you shall not be mentioned to a soul?" said David.

"I promise that faithfully."

"Well, Short and Presford lodged a complaint against you." David spoke slowly.

Powderdry was nervous. "Against me!" he exclaimed.

"Yes, against you. And they said that you must be discharged." David looked across the room.

"And you — you —" began Powderdry, fearing the worst.

"Well — ah —"

Powderdry thought it was true. He arose and gasped: "You don't mean to say, David, that you — you — Why, man, it would be ruin to me! I 've chased the phantom of politics until I 'm bankrupt, with only this salary to keep my family alive. It would be ruin, I tell you."

"They are the bosses, you know," said David, quite calmly.

"But you—did you—could you—say yes?"

"No, not exactly. I told them that they might go to the devil."

The effect was unnatural, but the major always was of an emotional temperament, and the tears seemed to come in spite of his gray hairs. He really cried, and David sat there with a smile on his face as if he enjoyed it.

"Come now, Powderdry," said he, coaxingly, "don't take on so. It's a very little matter. We've been brought down here as a pair of country bumpkins, and we've got to take care of ourselves. The trouble with you is that you talk too much. Just shut down on yourself. Politics is a game of bluff and silence, and the less you say and the calmer you look, the more you get."

The major's tears disappeared. "David, you are right."

"You have been saying some things about affairs here in town," continued the sheriff. "When you do that again, show discretion. If you are asked about the court-house crowd, don't use too many words. They might inconvenience you. Appear mysterious, and so forth, and so forth, and you will get the same effect. And about the sheriff's office, don't boast too much, but just say that Gad is attending to his work, and is refusing to play into the hands of the legal sharps, and mention a few instances where we have saved farmers. But while you are about it, put in a good word for Senator Boone, as the best friend the people ever had in the Legislature."

The bosses did not like Gad's independence. It injured their plans. It took away certain revenues that they had enjoyed. The mortgage-holders and note-shavers found that they no longer had a subservient tool. Colonel Short was especially sore. He did not have his usual monopoly of business. And yet David was wise enough to give him a share of it. Still, the circumstances were serious enough to cause Short and Presford to meet and talk over the situation.

But Sheriff Gad became remarkably circumspect in his conduct. He earned the respect and esteem of the town people, and as he spent much of his time in driving around the districts, the villagers and farmers soon got to know him better than any one else in the county. He was always polite, always attentive, and always willing to do any favors that were in his power. More than that, the country folks, when they came to town, found a good home-welcome at his house, and Ruth presided over the hospitalities with that grace and simplicity that charmed all her guests. She helped the women with their shopping, and pleased the men by her interest in their families. "The Gads are nice people," said the country visitors. "They are always glad to see us, and they are not uppish like the other folks in town."

And so matters went along through the summer. In the fall the campaign was unimportant, but in it Sheriff Gad was a worker. While the vote, as in all off years, was light elsewhere, the full party strength was polled in the upper districts, from which David had come.

In February the plans for the great election began, — the election of the county officers, including the clerk, whose term of office was six years. Candidates sprang up from every part of the county. By March there were enough to fill the places four times over. The bosses welcomed all, but showed no preferences. In April Sheriff Gad was invited to a conference at Colonel Short's office. Presford was there. So was Carr.

"We are going to have a big fight this fall," said Colonel Short, "the biggest fight we have ever had, and it looks to me that we must get as much new material on the ticket as we can. What do you think, Mr. Gad?"

"Oh, I 'm a new hand in politics, colonel," said David, deprecatingly. "These other gentlemen have more experience than I have. What do you think, Mr. Presford?"

"I prefer to bow to Colonel Short. He knows more about it than all the rest of us, I fear," declared Presford.

"In some way, I know not how," Colonel Short said, "the people in the county have got the idea that we folks in town are trying to run the party, and they seem to think that they ought to have a larger say in the management. Now I propose that we distribute the ticket so as to cover the county. To do that we should have to skip several districts, and as Sussex has had the sheriff's office for two years, I thought, Mr. Gad, that you might be willing to help us out."

David stopped twirling his thumbs, and glanced at the men before him.

"Do I understand, gentlemen, that the ticket is to be entirely new?"

"Well, mostly new,—as new as we can make it," replied Short.

"I suppose, Mr. Presford, that you will decline a renomination?"

The question was slyly put, and it almost staggered the conference.

"Well—ah—I will do what I can for the good of the party, Mr. Gad; but of course I shall remain in the hands of my friends."

Evidently Presford was embarrassed.

"Of course," said David, *sotto voce*.

"Now look here, Gad," put in Short, changing his manner, "give up this office for two years, and after that we 'll have something a great deal better for you."

David strangled the smile before it reached the surface.

"We gave this place—one of the best in the county—to you, you know."

"Yes, you did—you gave it freely—and the gift cost me twelve hundred and fifty dollars."

"We could n't help that," said the colonel; "it 's politics."

"Well," asked David again, "if I retire, what assurance will I have that you will remember your promise two years from now?"

"You have our word."

"Gentlemen, pardon me, but I don't like the security," said the sheriff as he arose. "I prefer to follow the example of Mr. Presford, and remain in the hands of my friends."

"That is base ingratitude," declared Colonel Short.

"No, colonel; it 's politics."

When David left, the door closed upon three silent men. They were in that somewhat uncomfortable state in which no one knows exactly what to say. The colonel arose, went to the window, and then turning suddenly, blurted out, —

"He 's a d—— fool."

"That 's what we get for putting such a dunce in politics," said Presford, as he threw his cigar in the coal-scuttle. "We 've imported him from the backwoods, and now he thinks that he is the biggest man in the county."

Carr, who had been a silent listener to everything, got up and jammed his hat on the back of his head.

"Carr, what do you think?" asked Short.

"I think," said Carr, musingly, "that you 've got a nice large white elephant named Gad on your hands, and that if you don't feed him well he 'll bu'st up your show."

David went directly home, and retired to his room. He sat by the window poring over a map, making notes, and jotting down names. Then, with his data, he threw himself on the bed. He did not sleep, but with his eyes wide open added occasionally to his memoranda. One hour afterwards he arose, and all the hard lines disappeared from his face. When he went downstairs he was buoyant and smiling.

" Been asleep ? " asked Ruth.

" No, dear ; just resting, and making out my route. I 've got to go away on business for several days."

" Senator Boone 's going away too, to-morrow, and Mrs. Boone was saying she did not know what she should do."

" Ask her to come and stay with you. I 'll go over after supper and take the invitation myself."

He went. The invitation was delivered and accepted. Presently the senator and David retired to the library. Their conference was long and earnest. David asked the fullest details of the boss management. Every trick, every resource, was explained by the senator.

"Now, senator," said David, "one more point. Will you go to the Senate again?"

"I will not make a contest for a nomination, nor will I spend anything for the election," he replied. "If the people want me, they can nominate and elect me. I'll deliver speeches and explain my views, but I won't pay a cent of blackmail to a lot of swindlers who call themselves managers."

"That's all I want to know," said David. "Just stick to that position and say nothing."

David started out the next morning bright and early. For nearly a week he was travelling from store to store, from house to house, from district to district. Everywhere he was holding conferences, and his invariable explanation of his visits was business. When he returned, Major Powderdry was sent out on another round of official duty. The people began to pour into town for their spring shopping, and the Gad house became their rendezvous. It made no difference how many visitors there were, Ruth always had room for more.

Weeks were passing, and it was drawing near the busy season of politics. The bosses laid aside their social exclusiveness and began their electioneering hospitality. Even the Presfords unbent, and little Dickey Binson was polite to everybody. Colonel Short and Mr. Presford made their tour of the county, but while they were well received, they seemed to miss something. They could not tell just what it was.

David doubled his activity. He was at a different church every Sunday, at the festivals and picnics and camp-meetings, saying little, but saying it well, and being generous when generosity was wise. If two events conflicted in the date, David was at one place, Powderdry at the other.

And so it went until the week before the primary election. David came back to town — "Come in, stranger," was the way Ruth welcomed him — and the political atmosphere was full of latent excitement. Boss Short, doubtful about something and suspicious of the possibility of a defection in the ranks, sent for Sheriff Gad.

"Tell the colonel that he can find me at home," was the reply to the messenger; but before the man got to the gate he rushed out and shouted, "Never mind, I 'm going down that way. It 's better for me to go," he added to himself.

When he entered Short's office he saw that the colonel was ill at ease. He himself was calm.

"Colonel," he said, after the civilities were exchanged, "I believe that you sent for me."

"Yes, Mr. Gad," replied Short, in his best voice. "We want to see what you will do for us if we let you have a renomination."

"In what way?"

"Well, the usual way, of course. You have n't been treating us fairly. You 've been sending business to Boone and Carr that ought to have come to me, and within the past eight weeks you have made me lose money by not acting at once in matters that I placed in your hands."

"My understanding, colonel, is that I am sheriff of the county, and not of any one person."

"Of course you are -- of course you are. You don't understand me; so let the matter drop. You want to be renominated. Now, you understand that! Well, you shall have it if you will help us with the rest of the ticket."

"I 'm much obliged to you, colonel, but I do not care for it." David said this quietly, but it had an enormous effect on the colonel. Losing his customary control, he jumped up and shouted, --

"Then what, in Heaven's name, do you want?"

"That 's my business," replied the sheriff.

"It shall be mine too," answered the colonel; "and if you do not help us out now, you 'll have to suffer for it."

"Don't bite off too much, you might not be able to chew it," said David, with great deliberation.

Short recovered his equipoise, and with evident sarcasm replied, "Thank you very much for your advice."

"Oh, you 're welcome;" and David bowed low and left the office.

On his way down the street he met Carr, who thanked him for having sent certain clients to his office. David drew him aside.

"Carr," he said, "if I were you I would keep hands off for the next few days. Take my advice and lay low; and don't say I told you."

Carr was a good lawyer, which is to say that he was a man of large policy and elaborate prudence.

David hurried home and resumed the work that he had left. He went over it carefully, and then, when he summed up his results, he took the names and figures over to Senator Boone. The Senator scanned them critically.

"It looks all right," he said.

But David did not rest with appearances. He was busy laying out new schemes, exhaustless in checkmating possible combinations of the court-house crowd.

The primaries were held. That night the news of them came to town. David was apparently unconcerned. Colonel Short and Mr. Presford were in doubt. They knew the men elected, but beyond that — nothing.

Following closely on the heels of the primaries came the convention. People from every section scented excitement, and they congregated in full force to see the fun. David was up at six o'clock. Ruth had laid in a heavy supply of food, with turkeys fat and tender, and home-made pies that pleased the taste so thoroughly that their indigestibility was forgiven.

Around the court-house groups began to gather. The roads leading to town pulsated with life. The streets became animated and noisy. Colonel Short's office had its doors wide open, with a welcome in the front room and a supply of demijohns in the rear. Mr. Presford paraded with his abundant politeness, and all the politicians and workers greeted the delegates with cordial handshakes and invitations to "wash the dust out of their throats."

The more Colonel Short canvassed the situation, the less he liked it. The delegates had come to town with ideas of what they wanted, and what they wanted did not harmonize with the court-house programme. His demand that Gad should be turned down met with little favor. The delegates did not go to his office to see him as they once did. He had to seek them. In his perturbation he ran against Mr. Presford.

"What does it mean?" Presford asked.

"What does what mean?"

"Why, all these fellows are conferring with Gad in the jury-room."

The time for the assembling of the convention arrived. Promptly the people filed into the big court-room and filled the benches. Delegates began to drop in. Reporters and secretaries took their seats. Everything was ready.

Just as the presiding officer rapped for order, Colonel Short, by a back stairway, entered the jury-room, and stood face to face with Sheriff Gad. The other people had gone to hear the proceedings.

Short motioned to Gad, and without a word both men stepped to the alcove of the window farthest from the door leading to the convention. Short jumped at once into the purpose of his call, and there was anger in his voice.

"I want to warn you, Mr. Gad, that if you attempt any of your tricks to-day you 'll suffer for them."

"Are you sure of it?" asked David.

"Yes; and if you have any prudence, you will take your renomination and help us out with our slate."

David put his thumbs in his vest and looked the colonel straight in the eye. "Colonel Short," he said, slowly and impressively, "you and your crowd are beaten out of your boots."

The usual self-control of the colonel disappeared. He flushed, and answered angrily, "I don't believe it."

"You 've got to believe it," said David, earnestly.

Short's brow darkened. He began to speak: "I say that you —"

But before he completed the sentence somebody opened the door, and just that instant a delegate called for cheers for Boone and Gad. The response that came, reinforced as it was by a cry of "Down with the note-shavers and up with honest men!" seemed to shake the building.

It shook it enough to break the slate that

Short thought he was holding in his hand, and to silence the insult that was trembling on his lips.

"If this is true, it 's trickery," he exclaimed, "it 's base ingratitude, and I 'll break up that convention if I have to die for it."

He started to go, but David got in his way, and laid his hands on him.

"No, you won't," he said.

"Take your hands off," Short shouted, hoarsely.

"If you go into that room, I 'll expose all the crookedness that has been going on in this court-house; I will, so help me God!"

Colonel Short staggered back to the alcove. "What do you mean?" he demanded.

"Never mind what I mean or what I know, but it is more than enough. The question is whether or not you want to get out of your wreck in decent shape. I don't want to be too hard on you. I 'm willing to do what I can for your man Stinson for sheriff, if you will let Carr, as your representative, nominate me."

Short's curiosity got the better of his anger.

"Nominate you? For what?" he asked.

"For clerk of the court," said David, quietly.

"For clerk of the court!" Short repeated, as if dumfounded. "Why, what 's to become of Presford?"

"I 'm sorry to say," replied David, with a calm, cool smile, "that Mr. Presford stands no more show in that convention than a morning-glory in a January blizzard."

People spoke of the convention as one of the most harmonious that they had ever known, and they always alluded to Carr's speech nominating David Gad as a masterpiece which was almost if not quite equal to the splendid address which Senator Boone delivered in accepting the nomination for the Senate as the representative of the people.

When David came to dinner on the day that he transferred himself from the shrievalty to the clerk's office, he found a feast.

"I thought you ought to have it," said Ruth, in reply to his compliments. "It shows how glad I am that we are fixed to stay in town for six years more."

"Well," said David, "you did it. If it had n't been for your good dinners and shopping trips with the country folks, we never could have won."

"How did you get along to-day?" asked Ruth.

"Splendidly. I appointed Powderdry my

chief deputy. The next thing I did was to discharge Dickey Binson, and I 've felt good ever since."

"How was Mr. Presford?"

"As polite as a preacher to a rich trustee. In fact, my dear, I really think that if the De Presfords should have another reception they would invite the De Gads."

It was the first time the matter had ever been mentioned by either of them. But Ruth understood it.

"And the De Gads," David went on, "would regret extremely that they were unable to accept the polite invitation of Mr. and Mrs. De Presford. That 's the way it runs, is n't it, Ruth?"

"Yes, David. At least, that 's what the 'Hand-Book of Etiquette' says."

www.ingramcontent.com/pod-product-compliance
Lightning Source LLC
Chambersburg PA
CBHW030836270326
41928CB00007B/1083
9783744714365